St Michael

Here's **H**ealth

CREATIVE
WHOLEFOODS

Front cover photographs show:
Main Picture: Layered Terrine (page 17) with Indian Black-eyed Beans (page 58), a salad of cucumber, French beans and celery, Strawberry and Pineapple Hazelnut Torte (page 75)
Left-hand Picture: Tomatoes with Continental Lentils (page 24)
Right-hand Picture: Ricotta Fingers (page 25)

Published 1986 by The Hamlyn Publishing Group Ltd, Bridge House, London Road, Twickenham, Middlesex

Copyright © Argus Health Publications Limited 1986

Photography by David Burch
Styling by Pip Kelly

ISBN 0 600 32668 3

Printed in Italy

CONTENTS

P 36 Smoked haddock pasta
58 black eyed beans (s) zagokra
Mexican beans
Turkish Partridge & parsnip
54 Stuffed boned Turkey (25)
" White nut stuffing
55 Duck Breasts in Orange
Smoked mack. dip

WHAT ARE WHOLEFOODS?

These are literally 'whole foods', or foods as near to their natural state as possible. Examples are wholemeal bread, flour, pasta and brown rice. Wholefoods are only refined or processed as much as is necessary to make them useful or edible and all the essential nutrients, such as protein, carbohydrate and fat, plus vitamins, minerals and fibre, which occur naturally in the food, are retained.

Why Use Wholefoods?

Wholefoods are preferred because they offer the best nutritional value per mouthful of food. For example, 100 per cent wholemeal flour contains valuable fibre, vitamins and minerals which are lost when the bran and wheatgerm are removed to make processed white flour. In the case of sugar, processing has removed all the minerals and trace elements which are found in less highly refined dark sugars. In both cases, the body would be better off obtaining energy from more complex foods that offer a variety of nutrients, rather than just calories.

Food needs to contain vitamins and minerals in order to be digested. Sugar and other refined foods, which do not have any of these nutrients, rob the body of those which should be busy elsewhere protecting and maintaining our health. Foods which contain their own vitamins and minerals make no such demands on the body. Wholefoods are digested more slowly than refined foods and so provide a steady stream of energy. Refined foods, on the other hand, especially sugar, cause rapid rises (and subsequent falls) in the blood sugar level and this can have a profound effect on our moods and general sense of well-being. Our 'engines' run better on these more complex foods.

Wholefoods thus are high in fibre and low in sugar – two important criteria for healthy eating. A healthy diet should also be low in fat and salt. Generally speaking, processed foods are high in both of these, as reading food labels will reveal. Briefly, the advice of medical experts is that we should be cutting down on the total amount of fat in our diet and making sure that at least two-thirds of the fat we do eat is high in polyunsaturates. Saturated fats – hard fats from animal sources, or hydrogenated vegetable fats – should be avoided as much as possible. There is no evidence to suggest that we need to eat saturated fat to be healthy. Indeed, the opposite seems to be the conclusion of most medical research. However, we do need some polyunsaturated fat in our diet because it contains essential fatty acids which the body cannot make, but which are essential for health.

The way we eat has been shown to have a direct effect on our health – not just making the difference between whether we have heart disease or diabetes, high blood pressure or gallstones, or are overweight (just some of the health problems associated with the typical British diet) but how we actually *feel* from day to day. Eat properly and we feel great! Eat poorly and we feel below par and lacking in essential vitality.

The Big Switch

To this end many of us have been making changes in the food we eat to include more high-fibre foods such as wholemeal bread, brown pasta and rice, pulses, whole cereals and grains, fresh fruit and vegetables. We have also tried to cut down on the amount of sugar by omitting it from tea and coffee, not sprinkling it on breakfast cereals, avoiding cakes, biscuits and sweets – making them treats rather than everyday foods. We have similarly attempted to cut down on fats by not adding them to cooked vegetables, spreading them thinly, cutting down on cakes and pastries, avoiding fried foods, switching to skimmed and semi-skimmed milks and using low-fat cheeses and yogurts.

We have also been steaming, poaching and grilling, rather than frying, and have become dab hands at stir-frying in a wok, using the minimum of oil. We have also cut down on the amount of fatty meats we eat, trimmed fat off meats and curtailed our use of hard and full-cream cheeses. But how many of us feel we have exhausted the possibilities and are now looking for new ways to develop a wholefood diet?

Why Creative Wholefoods?

Many people have become a little tired of basic wholefood cookery with its hearty crumbles and wholemeal pies, its muesli mountains and chunky slices and are now looking for something different. Many people, especially those with sedentary lifestyles, want lighter and smaller meals. People want food that is appetising and exciting to look at; food which offers new flavours or perhaps uses the flavours of foreign dishes tasted on holiday or at restaurants. We also want to know how to make the most of poultry and game, the latter being high in polyunsaturates and lower in fat than most meats.

To this end, *Creative Wholefoods* sets out to take us one stage on from the basics, giving new ideas for using fresh foods and leaner meats and fish. It also contains vegetarian suggestions because many people who are interested in a healthy diet, while not being vegetarian, are eating more non-meat meals.

Creative Wholefoods Ingredients

The raw ingredients are very important in every type of cooking, especially creative wholefood cookery. Try to obtain the freshest of fruit and vegetables, fish and meats. The fresher the food the better the flavour and the more nutrients we can expect it to contain. If food is fresh it speaks for itself. It does not need heavy sauces, rich with cream or flavourings, to give it character. You actually eat the food for its own flavour.

Using fresh foods and preparing them just before cooking and eating is a basic technique for healthy cooking and this style of preparation lends itself well to the wide range of ingredients used in *Creative Wholefoods*, drawn from the increasing number of once unusual ingredients now being imported.

As well as the unusual, you will also notice that some of the ingredients differ from standard cookbook ingredients. The following brief notes explain some of the more unusual raw materials used in this book.

Baking Powder

Where this is used, it is salt-free because this is another area where we can cut down on the sodium in our diet without any detrimental effect on the finished dish.

Carob

Most people like chocolate, but for some it means headaches, migraines, spots or other allergic reactions. (For all of us we know it should be an occasional treat only!) Carob offers a similar flavour to chocolate without the side-effects because it does not contain caffeine, theobromine, tyramine, phenylethylamine or oxalic acid – the substances that most commonly cause problems with chocolate.

Carob is available in powder form, just the same as cocoa (but, incidentally, without added sugar, salt or additives) and it is also available in bars, usually made with raw cane sugar. Some versions are also free from dairy produce (being made with soya). It can be used in the same way as chocolate in recipes. Like cocoa, carob powder must be stored in a dry place or it becomes hard.

Cheese

Making a little cheese go a lot further not only saves money but it also saves calories. Cheese is a very fatty food and contains saturated fat. In *Creative Wholefoods*, strongly flavoured mature cheeses are used so that smaller amounts are needed to obtain a good flavour. Low-fat soft cheeses such as quark or cottage cheese are used. You will be amazed to find that soft cheeses and yogurt can make excellent mousses (see page 76).

Coffee

Wherever a recipe calls for coffee, decaffeinated has been specified because caffeine has some side-effects that many people prefer to avoid. Decaffeinated coffee can be bought as instant granules, as ground coffee or as beans for grinding at home (for an extra fresh flavour).

Eggs

I always specify free-range eggs in my recipes and these are now available in many high street food stores and super-markets, as well as health food shops.

Flour

I always use 100 per cent wholemeal flour because it can achieve just as good results as white if you use the right cookery techniques. There is only one exception to this rule and that is for choux pastry which is more successful with 85 per cent wholemeal flour. Other flours such as barley, buckwheat and rye are made from whole grains, but they lack the protein content of wheat and so are not as successful for breads and cakes.

Fruit and Vegetables

Many people are concerned about the routine use of pesticides and other chemicals in modern farming and for this reason turn to organic produce where possible which is the result of chemical-free growing. The criteria which organic growers consider important are likely to be taste, texture and nutritional content.

Dried fruits are often coated with mineral oils and treated with sulphur dioxide to prevent them losing their natural colour. For this reason I use unsulphured or organically produced dried fruits. All dried fruit should be washed well in hot water and then dried thoroughly before use.

If you have to use canned fruit or vegetables try to obtain those canned in their own juice, or in fruit juice or water, without added salt or sugar.

Fructose

This may be new to some readers. It is the name for the sugar which occurs naturally in fruit. It is extracted to make a white sugar which is slightly granular. It should be used in smaller quantities than that of ordinary sugar because it is sweeter than sucrose. It has the additional benefit of being less disruptive to blood sugar levels which is why you will also see it being used in diabetic products.

Margarine and Butter

Unsalted butter is used in *Creative Wholefoods* both for its superior flavour and for its lack of salt. It also has better cooking characteristics than salted butter. Butter is an entirely natural product but it *is* a saturated fat.

Soft vegetable margarines are specified because these are higher in polyunsaturates than hard margarines which often contain a lot of animal fat. Generally the softer the margarine, the higher it is in polyunsaturates. Most brands will state if they are high in polyunsaturates.

Margarine does have its critics because it is made by a complicated chemical process and uses food additives such as emulsifiers, colourings and antioxidants. However, many *are* derived naturally. It is a question of reading the list of ingredients carefully to avoid any particular additive which you do not want to eat. Some margarines are made from cold-pressed oils which means less processing and some, available from health food shops, do not contain any colouring.

Beware of 'low-fat' and 'dairy' spreads; they may contain saturated, rather than unsaturated, fats. They contain a lot of water and so are unsuitable for cooking, especially frying, as they can spit dangerously. Butter and margarine both contain the same number of calories.

Meat

This book makes use of the leaner cuts of meat and the types likely to contain less saturated fat (see notes at the beginning of Chapter 4). It is worth mentioning that you do not have to give up meat to eat healthily. If you enjoy meat, you can just reduce the amount you eat and switch to the less fatty cuts and types. You can also employ techniques such as grilling and dry roasting which drain off excess fat.

Milk

Creative Wholefoods makes the most of skimmed and semi-skimmed milk because whole milk is one of the major sources of saturated fat in our diet. We still get most of the nutrients from skimmed milk that are in unskimmed milk, except for a little vitamin A and D. For most of us, however, these nutrients are well supplied elsewhere in our diet. They are found in green and orange vegetables and our skin manufactures vitamin D when exposed to sunlight. Pasteurised skimmed milk is now widely available from the milkman and from supermarkets.

Soya milk is an alternative favoured by some because it has about the same calorific value as standard (silver top) dairy milk but is low in fat and free from saturated fat. It can be used in some cooking, but does tend to curdle. It has a distinctive flavour and is also more expensive than cow's milk. It is mainly used by vegans and those who are allergic to lactose (milk sugar).

Oil

Little oil is used in these recipes, but good quality, cold-pressed vegetable oils are preferred to animal fats when cooking. Most of the savoury recipes use oil to sauté the vegetables and this can be olive oil, if you like the flavour, corn or soya oil. Keep safflower and sunflower oils for salad dressings as they are less stable at high temperatures.

Tofu

This is widely used in Japanese and Chinese cooking and is a vital source of protein in the Oriental diet. It is a curd made by coagulating soya milk and pressing it into curds in the same way that we coagulate dairy milk to make cheese. Bacteria culture, not rennet, is used, so strict vegetarians and vegans find tofu an acceptable product. It is very low in fat and high in protein so it is a valuable alternative to proteins used in the West such as meat, cheese and eggs which can contain a lot of fat. Tofu can also be used in sweet dishes to make cheesecakes and ice cream because it is very soft in consistency and bland in flavour.

Yogurt

Yogurt is a valuable aid in healthy cooking because it can replace cream for thickening savoury sauces, as well as replacing cream in sweet dishes. The newly available 'Greek-style' strained natural yogurts are especially useful for this and can even be made into piping creams. Mayonnaise-type salad dressings can be based on yogurt to provide a healthy alternative to the oil-based dressings and are popular with slimmers.

Wholemeal Bread
Whole recipe:
Calories 1250
Fat 22g
Fibre 34g

Although this book is about ways of making your wholefood cooking more creative and attractive, there is still a place for a few useful basic recipes on which you can build. A good wholemeal bread recipe and a reminder about the basics of wholemeal pastry never go amiss. And there are different types of pastry to consider, as we shall see.

Providing some basic recipes also gives those who are not new to cooking (but who might be new to some of the wholefood ingredients used) a good starting point for creative cookery. You can enjoy the recipes in the book and use the basics as a quick reference for a new way of more healthy eating.

As well as bread, there is a recipe for a basic wholemeal sponge – an area that gives lots of people difficulty. However, with the whisked sponge method you can achieve a lightness that escapes the traditional creamed sponge. And there is a delicious fruit cake made without added sugar, suitable for all sorts of family celebrations.

Wholemeal Bread and Rolls

WHOLEMEAL BREAD

MAKES 1 (450-g/1-lb) LOAF OR 8–10 ROLLS

350 g/12 oz wholemeal flour
pinch of sea salt
1 tablespoon vegetable oil
300 ml/½ pint lukewarm water
15 g/½ oz fresh yeast
1 (25-mg) vitamin C tablet
beaten egg or milk to glaze
poppy or sesame seeds
to decorate (optional)

∎

*Preparation time **15 minutes, plus about 40 minutes proving time***
*Cooking time **30 minutes***
*Oven temperature **230 C, 450 F, gas 8***

∎

1 Lightly grease a 450-g/1-lb loaf tin.
2 Sift the flour and salt into a mixing bowl, tipping in the residue of bran left in the sieve, and make a well in the centre.
3 Pour the oil into the water and crumble

in the yeast. Mix well.

4 Crush the vitamin C tablet to a powder and add to the yeast mixture.

5 Pour the liquid into the flour and mix to a dough. Knead lightly on a floured work surface for 5 minutes. Place the dough back in the mixing bowl and cover with a piece of oiled greaseproof paper. Leave to prove in a warm place until doubled in size (about 40 minutes).

6 Knock the dough back to remove air bubbles and knead again. Form into a sausage shape, fold the ends under and place in the prepared tin.

7 Cover with a clean tea-towel and leave until the dough has risen almost to the top of the tin. Brush with the beaten egg or milk, decorate with poppy or sesame seeds, if liked, and bake for 40 minutes.

8 The loaf is cooked when it falls easily from the tin and sounds hollow when tapped on the base.

You can add different flours to this recipe: replace one-third of the wholemeal flour with oat or rye flour, or use a malted Granary-type flour.

Variations

To make rolls, divide the dough into equal-sized pieces and shape each into a plait, a roll, or a loose knot, or any other suitable shape. Glaze, decorate with poppy or sesame seeds and place on a greased baking tray and bake for 20 minutes.

QUICK WHOLEMEAL BREAD

If in a hurry the bread does not have to be kneaded or allowed to prove. It can be shaped and placed straight into the tin and then covered and left to rise until it doubles in size, before being glazed and baked in the usual way. The result will be a closer textured but, nevertheless, tasty loaf. Add a little more water if making the bread by this method.

MELBA TOAST

You can make your own melba toast by toasting a slice of bread in the usual way then placing it flat on a bread board and cutting through it horizontally. Place the resultant two slices on a baking tray, or in a grill pan, and heat in the oven or under a moderate grill for 5–10 minutes to dry and curl the toast. Allow to cool completely, then store in an airtight tin.

CROÛTONS

These make an excellent accompaniment to soup. Garlic-flavoured croûtons can be used as an appetiser in place of salty and oily crisps and nuts.

Use a thickish slice of wholemeal bread. Cut away the crusts, which can be reserved for making breadcrumbs, then cube the bread. Heat a heavy-based pan over a moderate heat, without any added fat, and tip in the cubes of bread. Stir and turn until toasted all over. Alternatively, toast them in a grill pan. For a garlicy flavour, spread the bread thinly with a little garlic butter made by crushing 1–2 cloves of garlic and mashing them with unsalted butter, before cutting and toasting.

Melba Toast; Croûtons

WHOLEMEAL PASTRY

Wholemeal shortcrust pastry is made in the same way as regular pastry, using half fat to flour, and substituting 100 per cent wholemeal flour for the white flour. The flour should be sifted and the bran from the sieve returned to the flour. Rub in the fat until the mixture resembles breadcrumbs and then mix with cold water to a soft dough.

To make a lighter pastry, add 1 teaspoon baking powder to each 225 g / 8 oz flour. It is better to use salt-free baking powder, especially if you add salt to your pastry.

For shortcrust pastry you can use soft margarines or cooking fats which are high in polyunsaturates. Oil may also be used to make shortcrust pastry. Work it in with a fork instead of rubbing in the fat and proceed in the same way.

For a lower-fat pastry you can use the yeasted pastry recipe given in the recipe for Carrot and Watercress Pie on page 26. The pastry is made light and crisp by raising it with yeast and reducing the amount of fat. Another low-fat pastry is Choux Pastry. This is most successful with 85 per cent wholemeal flour rather than with 100 per cent.

Choux Pastry	
Whole recipe:	
Calories 1030	
Fat 70g	
Fibre 9g	

CHOUX PASTRY

Makes about 8 éclairs, 16 profiteroles, 1 Paris Brest gâteau or 1 gougère

150 ml/¼ pint water
50 g/2 oz unsalted butter
90 g/3½ oz 85 per cent wholemeal flour
2 free-range eggs, lightly beaten
50 g/2 oz Gruyère cheese, finely grated
(for gougère only)

■

Preparation time **15 minutes**
Cooking time **25 minutes**
Oven temperature **220 C, 425 F, gas 7**

1 Lightly grease a baking tray or an éclair tin. Have ready a piping bag fitted with a 1-cm/½-in plain nozzle.
2 Place the water and butter in a saucepan over a moderate heat until the butter melts.
3 Sift the flour, returning the bran to the flour (there will not be much compared with 100 per cent wholemeal flour).
4 Tip the flour, all in one go, into the butter and water and beat vigorously, with a wooden spoon, until the dough forms a smooth ball and leaves the sides of the pan to form a shiny lump.
5 Beat the eggs, one at a time, into the dough, beating well between each addition. Remove from the heat and beat in the cheese, if using.
6 Place the paste in the piping bag and pipe strips onto the tray or tin, cutting off the paste with a knife dipped in boiling water. Leave space between the éclairs if you are not using a special éclair tin. Alternatively, for profiteroles pipe 16 balls onto the baking tray, leaving a space between them.
7 Bake for 10 minutes, then reduce the temperature to 190 C, 375 F, gas 5 for a

Wholemeal Sponge	
Whole recipe:	
Calories 900	
Fat 52g	
Fibre 7g	

From left to right:
*Profiteroles filled with
strained natural yogurt;
Wholemeal Sponge;
Wholemeal Pastry Pie
Topping*

further 15 minutes, or until the éclairs or profiteroles are cooked and dry in the centre. Allow to become cold before filling.

This is a low-fat, light pastry which can be used for both sweet and savoury dishes. It is famous for making éclairs and profiteroles, but, for a change, try making a Paris Brest gâteau – a ring of choux pastry. Gougère is a savoury choux pastry dish – in this case add the grated Gruyère as instructed.

WHOLEMEAL
SPONGE

*40 g / 1½ oz unsalted butter or soft
vegetable margarine
75 g / 3 oz wholemeal flour
3 free-range eggs
50 g / 2 oz clear honey*

∎

Preparation time **10 minutes**
Cooking time **25–30 minutes**
Oven temperature **190 C, 375 F, gas 5**

1 Lightly grease and line with greased greaseproof paper a 17-cm/7-in cake tin.
2 Place the fat in a saucepan over a gentle heat and melt but do not allow to colour.
3 Sift the flour into a mixing bowl, returning the bran from the sieve to the flour.
4 Place the eggs and honey in the top of a double boiler, or in a basin standing over a pan of hot water, and whisk until thick and creamy or until the mixture will support your initials when written on the top in the mixture.
5 Using a large metal spoon, fold the flour into the mixture, working lightly but thoroughly. Add the melted fat by pouring in down the side of the bowl and folding in.
6 Pour into the prepared tin and bake for 25–30 minutes until firm and set and springy to the touch.

A basic sponge recipe is very useful for cakes and gâteaux and this one proves that you can make a very light sponge using wholemeal flour.

Instead of filling your wholemeal sponge with butter icing or cream why not use a yogurt-based piping cream? Try a no-added sugar jam or spread instead of regular jams which are high in sugar and often contain additives. A fresh or dried fruit purée mixed with strained yogurt, or a soft, white low-fat cheese, such as quark, also makes a good filling.

Wholemeal Pancakes	
1 pancake:	
Calories 50	
Fat 1g	
Fibre 1g	

WHOLEMEAL PANCAKES

MAKES 8

*100 g/4 oz wholemeal flour
pinch of sea salt (optional)
1 large, free-range egg (size 2)
300 ml/½ pint skimmed milk
a little corn or soya oil*

■

*Preparation time **5 minutes**
Cooking time **25 minutes***

■

1 Sift the flour into a mixing bowl, returning the bran from the sieve to the flour. Add the salt, if using and make a well in the centre of the flour.
2 Lightly beat the egg and place in the flour well.
3 Pour in a little milk and, using a fork, work the egg and milk into the flour, gradually combining more flour and adding the remaining milk as you whisk. Keep the paste smooth and avoid lumps by working gradually.
4 To make the pancakes, lightly grease a heavy based omelette pan or small frying pan with the oil and heat.

5 Pour in a little batter and tip the pan from side to side to coat the base of the pan with a thin, even layer. When set, slip a palette knife underneath and turn the pancake to cook for a minute on the other side.
6 If not using immediately, fold in half or pile the pancakes on top of each other and cover, to prevent them drying out. Keep in a warm place.

Very useful for sweet or savoury dishes. Try making them also with buckwheat flour or using half rye, maize or oat flour for a change.

WHOLEMEAL FRUIT CAKE

MAKES 1 (17-cm/7-in)
CAKE

*175 g/6 oz currants
200 g/7 oz sultanas
150 g/5 oz raisins
75 g/3 oz dried peaches, chopped
3 tablespoons concentrated apple juice
2 tablespoons brandy
75 g/3 oz stoneless dates, chopped
1 small cooking apple, peeled and chopped
2 tablespoons water
1 ripe banana, mashed
175 g/6 oz soft vegetable margarine
4 free-range eggs
175 g/6 oz wholemeal flour
2 teaspoons salt-free baking powder
½ teaspoon freshly grated nutmeg
½ teaspoon ground cinnamon
100 g/4 oz ground almonds
100 g/4 oz whole unblanched almonds, finely chopped
12 pecan nut halves to decorate*

■

*Preparation time **40 minutes, plus overnight soaking**
Cooking time **2 hours**
Oven temperature **150 C, 300 F, gas 2***

■

1 The day before, prepare the first four ingredients by washing and drying well

Wholemeal Pancakes

Wholemeal Fruit Cake

and placing in a bowl with 2 tablespoons of the apple juice and the brandy. Cover and leave overnight, stirring a few times.

2 Next day, lightly grease and line with a double thickness of greaseproof paper a 17-cm/7-in deep cake tin.

3 Place the dates and apple in a saucepan with the remaining apple juice and the water and simmer to a purée. Allow to cool.

4 Place the banana in a mixing bowl and cream well with the margarine and the date and apple purée until the mixture is light and well mixed.

5 Lightly beat the eggs and add them one at a time to the creamed mixture, beating well between additions.

6 Sift the flour with the baking powder and the spices and, returning the bran from the sieve to the flour, fold in.

7 Fold in the ground almonds.

8 Fold in the soaked fruit and chopped almonds and place the mixture in the prepared tin. Smooth and level the top and arrange the pecan nuts around the edge of the cake. Bake for 2 hours. The cake is cooked when a skewer inserted in the centre comes out clean. With experience you will be able to tell when your cake is cooked without puncturing the top. Cover the cake with a double layer of greaseproof paper when it reaches the desired colour – usually after about $1-1\frac{1}{4}$ hours. The top will become burnt if it is not covered. Allow to cool for 30 minutes in the tin, then transfer to a wire rack to cool completely.

This is a rich, but versatile cake for all occasions. It has no added sugar, but derives its sweetness from the banana, dried fruits and concentrated apple juice. For best results cook in a good, heavy tin. I find non-stick baking tins are too thin for cooking a cake for a long time and will lead to burnt base and sides if not well lined or cooked at a very slow temperature. This problem can be alleviated by tying a double layer of newspaper or brown paper around the sides of the tin before cooking.

Wholemeal Fruit Cake
Whole recipe:
Calories 5500
Fat 313g
Fibre 106g

VEGETARIAN DISHES: APPETISERS AND MAIN COURSES

All the recipes in this section are vegetarian and they range from simple snacks and appetisers to main courses.

Many people claim that the vegetarian way of eating is better for us than eating meat, but just avoiding meat or fish (or eggs, cheese and milk in the case of strict vegetarians and vegans) does not in itself make for a healthier diet. The best vegetarian diets are also wholefood diets — that is they aim to be high in fibre and low in fat, sugar and salt. To ensure protein intake is sufficient, vegetarians also need to combine two of three basic vegetarian protein-rich foods at one meal during the day. They will then be obtaining protein with fibre and without the fat found in meat. The groups are (1) pulses (i.e. beans, chickpeas, lentils etc.) (2) cereals (i.e. grains such as wheat and wheat products such as bread and pasta plus whole grains such as rice, rye, barley, oats etc.), nuts and seeds.

Adding dairy products to the above foods will enhance the value of the protein, but there is a tendency for vegetarians to rely too much on dairy produce, so this is a point to watch if you are eating a vegetarian diet.

Layered Terrine

Layered Terrine
Per portion:
Calories 140
Fat 10g
Fibre 2g

LAYERED TERRINE

SERVES 10
AS A STARTER

Layer 1
225 g/8 oz mushrooms
2 teaspoons oil
150 g/5 oz leek, finely diced
150 ml/¼ pint vegetable stock
3 teaspoons powdered gelatine or
1 teaspoon agar agar
pinch of paprika

Layer 2
1 large avocado (about 400 g/14 oz)
juice of ½ lemon
175 g/6 oz feta cheese

Setting agent
3 teaspoons powdered gelatine or 1
teaspoon agar agar
4 tablespoons boiling water

Layer 3
225 g/8 oz smoked tofu
juice of ½ lemon
100 g/4 oz quark (low-fat soft cheese)

■

Preparation time 1½ hours

1 Wipe the mushrooms and place 175 g/6 oz in a food processor and chop very finely. Heat the oil in a frying pan and add the mushrooms and leek. Cover and sweat for 10 minutes.

2 Bring the stock to the boil in a small pan. Remove from the heat and sprinkle over the gelatine, stirring until dissolved. If using agar agar, see Note.

3 Place the vegetables in a food processor or liquidiser and blend to a purée. Stir in the stock and paprika and mix throughly.

4 Slice the remaining mushrooms and place in the bottom of a large terrine. Pour the mushroom purée on top, level and place in a freezer for 20 minutes to set.

5 Make the second layer. Peel the avocado and remove the stone. Roughly chop the flesh and place in a food processor or liquidiser with the lemon juice and feta cheese. Process to a purée.

6 Prepare the setting agent for layers two and three by sprinkling the gelatine onto the water and stirring until dissolved or follow the instructions for agar agar.

7 Pour half the dissolved setting agent into the avocado purée and mix thoroughly. When the mushroom layer is firm enough, pour the avocado layer on top and return to the freezer for 15 minutes to set.

8 For the third layer, chop the tofu into a food processor or liquidiser, reserving about 2 tablespoons. Cut the reserved tofu into small dice. Blend the tofu in the processor to a purée with the lemon juice and quark. Blend in the rest of the setting agent and then fold in the diced tofu.

9 When the avocado layer has set, pour the tofu mixture on top. Smooth and leave in the refrigerator to set.

10 To serve, cut slices from the terrine and place on individual serving dishes. Serve with wholemeal melba toast (see page 11).

This exotic vegetarian dish can be used as a starter or a main course. There are many recipes for layered pâtés and terrines, but some are soft and difficult to handle. This recipe combines colours and flavours successfully and also keeps the pâté firm and manageable by using a setting agent.

In this recipe I have used gelatine because of its convenience and because it assures success. But, as gelatine is an animal product, for a truly vegetarian dish you might prefer to use agar agar – a setting agent derived from seaweed. Instead of sprinkling onto hot water, agar agar is sprinkled onto *cold* water and then brought to boiling point in a saucepan. Stir the mixture all the time as you heat it. I find less agar agar than gelatine is needed to set the same amount of liquid. Manufacturers usually recommend 2 teaspoons to set 600 ml/1 pint, but I only use 1 teaspoon or the set is too rubbery.

Stuffed Peppers;
Avocado Gratin

Avocado Gratin

Per portion:

Calories 260

Fat 25g

Fibre 3g

Avocado Gratin

SERVES 4

2 ripe avocados (about 400 g/14 oz
each)
2 tablespoons strained natural yogurt
1 teaspoon lemon juice
½ grapefruit, pink if possible
75 g/3 oz roasted cashew nuts, salted if
liked
lemon slices to garnish

■

Preparation time 15 minutes
Cooking time 15 minutes
Oven temperature 200 C, 400 F, gas 6

■

1 Have ready a non-stick baking tray or
an ovenproof dish that will contain the
four avocado halves.
2 Halve the avocados and remove the
stones. Scoop out the flesh, leaving just
enough to keep the avocado shells rigid.
Roughly chop the flesh and place in a food
processor or liquidiser with the yogurt.
Blend to a purée. Brush the avocado shells
with the lemon juice to prevent any
discoloration.
3 Halve the grapefruit and skin the
segments, if liked, or leave the skin on.
Cut each segment into two or three
equal-sized pieces.
4 Mix the nuts, grapefruit and purée
together and pile back into the shells.
5 Place on the baking tray or in the dish
and bake for 10–15 minutes. Serve in
individual avocado dishes, each garnished
with a slice of lemon.

Avocado is a popular starter and this is an
unusual way of serving it. Although it is
nice warm, this dish may also be served
cold for a refreshing summer lunch. Serve
with wholemeal melba toast.

STUFFED PEPPERS

Serves 6 as a starter, 3 as a main course

*3 peppers, red, green or a mixture of both
50g/2oz buckwheat
100g/4oz frozen spinach, defrosted
100g/4oz mushrooms, sliced
1 teaspoon ground cumin
parsley sprigs to garnish (optional)*

■

*Preparation time **20 minutes**
Cooking time **15 minutes**
Oven temperature **180C, 350F, gas 4***

■

1 Have ready an ovenproof dish in which the halved peppers can sit comfortably side by side.
2 Blanch the whole peppers in boiling water for 5 minutes. Drain and refresh under cold water. Halve them across, cutting through the stalk and discarding the seeds and pith inside, but leaving the stalks in position. Place in the prepared dish.
3 Boil the buckwheat for 10 minutes, drain and return to the saucepan.

4 Add the thawed spinach, mushrooms and cumin to the saucepan and stir over a low heat for a few minutes.
5 Pile the mixture into the pepper shells and bake for 15 minutes. Serve individually or on one or more large plates, garnished with sprigs of parsley, if liked.

Red or green peppers can be used for this dish. Red are sweeter but a mixture of the two looks good, giving a contrast of colours when serving. Substitute other whole grains such as millet or cracked wheat (bulghur) for a change.

GOAT'S CHEESE DIP

SERVES 8

*100g/4oz well-flavoured goat's cheese
2 spring onions, chopped
1 teaspoon wholegrain mustard
freshly ground black pepper
2 teaspoons lemon juice
225g/8oz quark (low-fat soft cheese)
2 free-range egg whites*

■

*Preparation time **5 minutes***

■

1 Have ready two large ramekins or one serving dish.
2 Place the goat's cheese in a food processor or liquidiser and add the chopped spring onions, the mustard, pepper, lemon juice and quark and blend together well.
3 Whisk the egg whites until stiff but not dry and fold into the cheese mixture.
4 Place in the ramekins or dish and chill until ready to serve.

This mousse-type dip is a delicious way to use the tangy flavour of goat's cheese which is enhanced by the spring onions. It is delicious with crudités or on crisp rolls, toast or other wholemeal crackers or crispbreads.

Stuffed Peppers	
Per portion:	
Starter:	
Calories 45	
Fat trace	
Fibre 2g	
Main Course:	
Calories 90	
Fat 1g	
Fibre 4g	

Goat's Cheese Dip

Goat's Cheese Dip	
Per portion:	
Calories 75	
Fat 4g	
Fibre 0g	

Cheese Croquettes

Per croquette:

Calories 80	
Fat 2g	
Fibre Ig	

It is not absolutely necessary to chill the croquettes if all the ingredients came straight from the refrigerator.

From left to right:
Cheese Croquettes;
Spinach Soufflé;
White Nut Croquettes

CHEESE CROQUETTES

MAKES 6

100 g / 4 oz cottage cheese
1 small carrot, grated
75 g / 3 oz mushrooms, finely diced
2 spring onions, sliced
2 teaspoons chopped fresh basil
100 g / 4 oz curd cheese
25 g / 1 oz sesame seeds

■

*Preparation time **10 minutes***
*Cooking time **30 minutes***

■

1 Sieve the cottage cheese into a bowl.
2 Add the carrot, mushrooms, spring onion, basil and curd cheese; mix well.
3 Place the sesame seeds on a plate or flat board. Take small handfuls of the cheese mixture and roll them into croquette shapes. Lightly roll in the sesame seeds and place on a serving plate.
4 Chill in the refrigerator.

These croquettes are rather soft and delicate to handle, but they look very nice and taste even better. Serve on a bed of lettuce with some wholegrain crisp rolls or crispbread. Use black or white sesame seeds, or roll half in white and half in black seeds.

SPINACH SOUFFLÉ

SERVES 4

50 g / 2 oz soft vegetable margarine
50 g / 2 oz wholemeal flour
300 ml / ½ pint skimmed milk
50 g / 2 oz Gruyère cheese, grated
175 g / 6 oz frozen spinach, defrosted, or
450 g / 1 lb fresh, cooked and chopped
freshly grated nutmeg
freshly ground black pepper
4 free-range eggs, separated

■

Preparation time **15 minutes**
Cooking time **40 minutes**
Oven temperature **190 C, 375 F, gas 5**

■

1 Prepare an 18-cm/7-in soufflé dish by lightly greasing and dusting with flour.
2 Melt the fat in a large saucepan and add the flour. Stir over a low heat until smooth. Gradually add the milk, stirring continuously to prevent lumps forming.
3 Stir in the cheese and the spinach, then season to taste with nutmeg and pepper.
4 Remove from the heat and lightly beat the egg yolks into the mixture.
5 Whisk the egg whites until stiff but not dry. Mix in 2 tablespoons to lighten the mixture, then fold in the remainder and pour into the prepared dish.
6 Bake for 35–40 minutes until well risen and set inside. This is when an inserted skewer comes out clean.
7 Serve immediately.

WHITE NUT CROQUETTES

MAKES 10

100 g / 4 oz cashew nut pieces
100 g / 4 oz brazil nuts, roughly chopped
75 g / 3 oz wholemeal breadcrumbs
2 teaspoons chopped fresh dill
1 free-range egg
1 tablespoon vegetable purée
dill sprig to garnish

■

Preparation time **10 minutes**
Cooking time **20 minutes**
Oven temperature **160 C, 325 F, gas 3**

■

1 Have ready a lightly greased or non-stick baking tray.
2 Place the cashews and brazil nuts in a food processor and grind them until they are still a little 'nutty' and not as well milled as ground almonds.
3 Add the remaining ingredients to the food processor and process until they are combined and sticking together.
4 Take small handfuls from the processor and form into croquettes, rolling lightly on a board and levelling the ends.
5 Place on the baking tray and bake at the top of the oven (or the hottest part) for 20 minutes. Serve hot or cold garnished with a sprig of dill.

Fresh dill gives these croquettes their aromatic flavour. The vegetable purée can be bought from health food shops or delicatessens.

If using fresh spinach in the soufflé, wash well and place in a saucepan without any additional water and cook for 3–5 minutes, turning the spinach to prevent it sticking. Remove from the heat, drain well and chop very finely on a chopping board or in a food processor.

Spinach Soufflé	
Per portion:	
Calories 300	
Fat 20g	
Fibre 4g	

White Nut Croquettes	
Per croquette:	
Calories 140	
Fat 12g	
Fibre 2g	

Tomato Tortilla
Per portion:
Calories 210
Fat 13g
Fibre 2g

*Baked Aubergine Slices;
Tomato Tortilla;
Gazpacho*

To peel tomatoes, make a cross in the skin of each tomato with a sharp knife and place the tomatoes in boiling water for 30 seconds. The skins should peel off easily. Transfer the tomatoes to a bowl of cold water before chopping, if required.

TOMATO TORTILLA

SERVES 8

*450g/1 lb 'waxy' potatoes
4 tablespoons olive oil
8 free-range eggs
1 (397-g/14-oz) can tomatoes, drained
and roughly chopped
sea salt
freshly ground black pepper*

Preparation and cooking time
25–30 minutes

■

1 Scrub the potatoes, but do not peel, and boil for 10–15 minutes until almost soft. Drain and, when cool enough to handle, cut into small dice.
2 Heat the oil in an omelette pan. Add the potato pieces and sauté until cooked through.
3 Beat the eggs in a basin and add the

tomatoes and salt and pepper to taste. Pour the eggs over the potatoes in the pan and stir round with a wooden spoon or spatula until the mixture is almost set. Neaten the edges and leave the omelette to cook for a few minutes.

4 Invert onto a plate and serve at once or allow to become completely cold and then cut into wedges.

Tortilla is a deep Spanish omelette that is cut like a cake. It can be served hot or cold and makes a good accompaniment to salad, or can be used as a snack in its own right. Serve on a bed of crisp green salad and garnish with green olives.

BAKED AUBERGINE SLICES

SERVES 8

1 (2.5-cm/1-in) piece fresh root ginger
2 cloves garlic, crushed
1 teaspoon paprika
225 g/8 oz tomatoes, peeled and chopped
2 shallots, chopped
2 large aubergines
1 tablespoon vegetable oil
300 ml/½ pint vegetable stock

■

*Preparation time **20 minutes, plus overnight marination***
*Cooking time **40 minutes***
*Oven temperature **180 C, 350 F, gas 4***

■

1 Have ready a 23-cm/9-in diameter ovenproof dish.
2 Grate the ginger and mix with the garlic and paprika.
3 Add the chopped tomatoes and shallots and stir well.
4 Slice the aubergines into 1-cm/½-in rounds and toss well in the mixture of vegetables and spices. Place the aubergines and vegetable mixture in the dish, cover and marinate overnight in the refrigerator.
5 Next day place the oil in a deep pan and

heat. Sauté the aubergine mixture in this, turning frequently, for about 10 minutes.
6 Add the stock, cover and simmer. Transfer to the dish and bake, covered, for about 40 minutes.

GAZPACHO

SERVES 6

450 g/1 lb fresh ripe tomatoes
1 cucumber, chopped
2 shallots, diced
1 red pepper, deseeded and diced
2 cloves garlic, crushed
600 ml/1 pint tomato juice
3 drops Tabasco sauce
2 tablespoons olive oil
1 tablespoon white wine vinegar
sea salt (optional)
1–2 tablespoons chopped parsley

■

*Preparation time **12–15 minutes***
*Cooking time **1 hour***

■

1 Peel the tomatoes, see Note opposite, and roughly chop the flesh into a food processor or liquidiser.
2 Add all the remaining ingredients except the salt and parsley and blend to a purée.
3 Adjust the seasoning, adding more Tabasco, if you like it hot, sea salt to taste and half the chopped parsley.
4 Transfer to a sealed container in the refrigerator for an hour then whisk again just before serving. Sprinkle with the remaining parsley and a few of the chopped vegetables, if desired, to garnish.

Serve with bowls of diced peppers, onions and Croûtons (see page 11) or Garlic Toast (see page 32).

Gazpacho

Per portion:

Calories 80

Fat 5g

Fibre 2g

Baked Aubergine Slices

Per portion:

Calories 30

Fat 2g

Fibre 2g

Tomatoes with
Continental Lentils

**Tomatoes with
Continental Lentils**

Per portion:

Calories **75**

Fat **4g**

Fibre **4g**

TOMATOES WITH CONTINENTAL LENTILS

SERVES 8

*8 large beefsteak tomatoes
100g/4oz whole green lentils
1 bay leaf
2 tablespoons olive oil
2–3 teaspoons white wine or cider
vinegar
1 teaspoon wholegrain mustard
freshly ground black pepper
2 cloves garlic, crushed
parsley sprigs to garnish*

■

*Preparation time **20 minutes**
Cooking time **10–15 minutes**
Oven temperature **180C, 350F, gas 4***

1 Have ready an ovenproof dish in which the tomatoes can sit comfortably side by side.

2 Wash the lentils and boil with the bay leaf in plenty of water for 15-20 minutes or until cooked, but still whole. Drain and remove the bay leaf.

3 Cut the tops from the tomatoes, retaining them to use as lids. Using a serrated knife such as a grapefruit knife, cut out the seeds and pulp and discard. Turn the tomatoes upside down to drain off any excess liquid.

4 Place the oil, vinegar, mustard, pepper and garlic in a clean screwtop jar and shake vigorously to combine. Toss the lentils in this dressing and pile into the tomato shells.

5 Replace the tomato lids and bake the tomatoes for 10–15 minutes. Garnish with sprigs of parsley.

Ricotta Fingers

RICOTTA FINGERS

MAKES 20

100 g / 4 oz wholemeal flour
7 g / ¼ oz fresh yeast
4½ tablespoons lukewarm water
75 g / 3 oz frozen spinach, defrosted and drained
175 g / 6 oz ricotta cheese
sea salt
freshly ground black pepper
beaten egg or milk to glaze
watercress sprig to garnish (optional)

■

*Preparation time **15 minutes, plus 45–60 minutes proving time***
*Cooking time **12 minutes***
*Oven temperature **200 C, 400 F, gas 6***

■

1 Sift the flour into a mixing bowl.
2 Crumble the yeast into the water and add to the flour to form a soft dough. Knead for 2 minutes, then cover and leave until doubled in size, about 45–60 minutes.
3 Lightly grease a baking tray.
4 Place the spinach and cheese in a food processor or liquidiser with seasoning to taste and purée until smooth.
5 Knock back the dough and roll out into a rectangle about 30 × 17 cm / 12 × 7 in. Place strips of the spinach mixture across the pastry at 1-cm / ½-in intervals. Cut the pastry into 10 strips across and moisten the edges of the cuts with water or beaten egg. Fold the pastry over to make fingers and cut each in half to make 20 fingers in all. Glaze and bake on the prepared tray for 12 minutes. Serve garnished with a sprig of watercress, if liked.

Yeasted pastry is used in this recipe. It makes a light and risen wholemeal pastry without the fat needed for wholemeal shortcrust or other forms of pastry.

Ricotta Fingers	
Per finger:	
Calories 35	
Fat 1g	
Fibre 1g	

Carrot and Watercress Pie

Carrot and Watercress Pie	
Per portion:	
Calories 280	
Fat 9g	
Fibre 9g	

CARROT AND WATERCRESS PIE

SERVES 8

Pastry
350 g/12 oz wholemeal flour
75 g/3 oz unsalted butter or soft
vegetable margarine
150 ml/¼ pint lukewarm water
15 g/½ oz fresh yeast
beaten egg or milk to glaze

Carrot Layer
225 g/8 oz carrots
1 (425-g/15-oz) can butter beans or
100 g/4 oz dried butter beans, soaked
and cooked (see Note)
2 teaspoons caraway seeds
¼ teaspoon freshly grated nutmeg
sea salt
freshly ground black pepper

Watercress Layer
275 g/10 oz potatoes
¼ teaspoon Vecon (concentrated
vegetable stock)
4½ tablespoons hot water
about 100 g/4 oz watercress
2 shallots, finely grated

Carrot and Watercress Pie

If using dried butter beans soak them overnight then rinse. Bring to the boil and boil hard for 10 minutes. Reduce the heat and simmer for 30–45 minutes until soft.

Preparation time **50–60 minutes**
Cooking time **30 minutes**
Oven temperature **200 C, 400 F, gas 6**

■

1 Lightly grease a raised pie tin, terrine dish or large loaf tin.

2 To make the pastry, sift the flour into a mixing bowl, returning the bran to the flour, and rub in the fat until the mixture resembles fine breadcrumbs.

3 Place the warm water in a jug and crumble in the yeast. Stir well, then pour onto the flour and mix to a dough. Knead lightly on a floured worktop to make a soft dough. Cover the pastry and leave to rest while you prepare the filling.

4 To make the carrot layer, scrub or peel the carrots and halve lengthways. Boil or steam them for 10 minutes, until just cooked.

5 Place in a food processor or liquidiser with the butter beans and purée until smooth. Tip into a bowl and add the spices and seasoning to taste.

6 To make the watercress layer, scrub the potatoes and coarsely chop. Boil or steam for about 15 minutes, until cooked.

7 Drain the potatoes and mash with a fork. Dissolve the Vecon in the water and cream into the potato.

8 Finely chop the watercress (reserving a few sprigs to garnish) and add to the potato. Stir in the shallots.

9 Roll out the pastry and line the prepared tin or dish, then re-roll the pastry and cut a lid to fit. Cut strips to fit around the top of the tin or dish and stick these onto the pastry edge to form a lip onto which the lid may be sealed.

10 Place the carrot layer in the base of the pie case and the watercress layer on top.

11 Seal the lid in place with a little beaten egg and flute the edges of the pie. If liked, decorate the top of the pie with pastry trimmings cut into decorative shapes.

12 Glaze and bake for 30 minutes. Serve garnished with the reserved watercress sprigs.

GRAPEFRUIT SALAD

SERVES 8

50 g/2 oz green beans
1 pink grapefruit
2 tablespoons olive oil
2 teaspoons lemon juice
freshly ground black pepper
4 sticks celery, sliced
½ cucumber, sliced

■

*Preparation time **20 minutes***

■

1 Trim the beans, then blanch for 3 minutes. Drain and refresh under cold water and slice each bean into three.
2 Peel the grapefruit and cut away all the skin from the segments – do this over a bowl to catch the juice. Chop the grapefruit segments into smaller pieces.
3 Whisk the grapefruit juice with the oil, lemon juice and pepper to taste, then toss in all the salad ingredients.
6 Chill until required. Garnish with any reserved celery leaves you may have.

STUFFED CRÊPES

SERVES 6

1 quantity wholemeal pancakes (page 14)
apple slices and walnut halves for decoration (optional)
Filling
225 g/8 oz cottage cheese
50 g/2 oz stoneless dates, chopped
50 g/2 oz walnuts, chopped
1 dessert apple, diced
juice of ½ lemon
freshly ground black pepper

■

*Preparation time **10 minutes***
*Cooking time **15–20 minutes, plus time to make the pancakes***

■

1 Have ready 6 cold pancakes (the recipe on page 14 makes about 8).
2 Mix together all the ingredients for the filling, place a spoonful on each pancake and roll up.
3 Decorate the tops of the rolled pancakes with slices of apple and walnut halves, if liked.

Grapefruit Salad
Per portion:
Calories 40
Fat 8g
Fibre 1g

Stuffed Crêpes
Per portion:
Calories 120
Fat 6g
Fibre 2g

Grapefruit Salad; Stuffed Crepes

FISH DISHES

Fish has lots on offer for a healthy diet. It is a good source of easily digestible protein and is low in fat. Much of the fat that is found in fish is high in polyunsaturates, unlike that found in meat. A special substance in fish oil, called EPA, has also been found to help stop the blood clumping together, or becoming sticky, which is thought to be a contributory factor in heart disease. The old wives' tale that fish is good for the brain may have some foundation in fact because substances found in fish have been found to cross into the brain, suggesting some special function there.

Fish is also the ultimate convenience food. It takes only 10 minutes to grill or steam fish and 15 minutes to poach it in the oven. It can be wrapped in paper or foil and be cooked 'en papillotte' in the oven where it will cook in its own juices.

There is no need to add fat during cooking, especially with naturally oily fish such as herring and mackerel. Forget about the batter and the chips and enjoy fish for its own flavour!

Court Bouillon

COURT BOUILLON

MAKES 1 litre/2 pints

2 carrots, quartered
1 onion, quartered
2 sticks celery, each cut into 2–3 pieces
2 shallots, halved · 1 bay leaf
3 sprigs parsley stalks · 2 sprigs thyme
6 black peppercorns
juice of $\frac{1}{2}$ lemon
300 ml/$\frac{1}{2}$ pint dry white wine
900 ml/1$\frac{1}{2}$ pints water

■

*Preparation time **10 minutes***
*Cooking time **20 minutes***

■

1 Place all the ingredients in a large saucepan and bring to the boil. Lower the heat and simmer for 20 minutes.
2 Strain and allow to cool before storing in the refrigerator. This stock also freezes well.

Sprats with Stir-fried
Cabbage

SPRATS WITH STIR-FRIED CABBAGE

SERVES 2

*350 g/12 oz sprats or sardines
juice of 1 lemon
freshly ground black pepper
1 tablespoon sesame oil
$\frac{1}{2}$ green pepper, deseeded and sliced
2 spring onions, sliced into rounds
350 g/12 oz greens or curly kale, finely
sliced or shredded
1 tablespoon brown rice vinegar
1 tablespoon tamari or shoyu sauce
lemon twists to garnish*

■

*Preparation time **20 minutes**
Cooking time **7 minutes***

1 Cut the sprats by slipping a knife from the tail end to the head and pulling out the guts and gills. This is best done at the sink under cold running water.
2 Pat the fish dry with absorbent kitchen paper and place in a grill pan. Pour the juice of the lemon over the fish and sprinkle with freshly ground black pepper. Grill under a moderate heat for about 7 minutes, turning the fish once, until cooked through.
3 While the sprats are cooking, stir-fry the vegetables. Heat the oil in a large frying pan or wok and add the pepper and spring onion. Stir-fry for 1 minute, then add the greens and continue to stir-fry.
4 Add the rice vinegar and tamari or shoyu and finish the cooking. It should take about 5 minutes at the most. Serve garnished with lemon twists.

Sprats with Stir-fried Cabbage	
Per portion:	
Calories 330	
Fat 23g	
Fibre 7g	

Poached Salmon	
100g steak:	
Calories 160	
Fat 10g	
Fibre 0g	
175g steak:	
Calories 280	
Fat 17g	
Fibre 0g	

From top to bottom:
Prawn Paella;
Tuna Tomatoes;
Poached Salmon

POACHED SALMON

SERVES 4

4 (100–175 g / 4–6 oz) salmon steaks
600 ml / 1 pint court bouillon (page 28)
quartered lemon slices to garnish

■

Preparation time **2 minutes, plus time to make the court bouillon if necessary**
Cooking time **15 minutes**
Oven temperature **180 C, 350 F, gas 4**

■

1 Place the fish in an ovenproof dish. Bring the court bouillon to boiling point and pour over the fish.
2 Poach gently for 15 minutes and serve at once with an endive salad, garnished with quartered lemon slices.

PRAWN PAELLA

SERVES 4

175 g / 6 oz long-grain brown rice
2 tablespoons olive oil
2 cloves garlic, crushed
2 onions, diced (use red onions if you can obtain them)
1 red pepper, deseeded and diced
1 teaspoon turmeric
175 g / 6 oz green beans
4 tomatoes, quartered
900 ml / 1½ pints vegetable or fish stock
225 g / 8 oz peeled cooked prawns, defrosted if frozen
100 g / 4 oz frozen or fresh peas

■

Preparation time **15 minutes**
Cooking time **40 minutes**

■

1 Wash the rice and boil for 15 minutes.
2 Oil a paella pan or large frying pan and gently sauté the garlic, onion and pepper for 5 minutes. Do not brown the vegetables, just soften them.
3 Add the turmeric and the rice and cook for 3–4 minutes, stirring gently.
4 Arrange the beans in the centre of the pan and place the tomatoes around the edge, leaving a gap around the outside of the beans in which to place the peas and prawns.
5 Pour on the stock and leave to cook, without stirring, for 20 minutes.
6 Add the prawns and peas and continue cooking for a further 10 minutes, adding more vegetable stock as necessary to prevent the mixture drying out. Do not add too much stock as the rice should have absorbed all the liquid at the end of the cooking time.

TUNA TOMATOES

SERVES 4

50 g / 2 oz brown rice
4 large beefsteak tomatoes, about 175 g / 6 oz each
1 (198-g / 7-oz) can tuna fish in brine or tomato juice, drained
1 (142-g / 5-oz) can sweetcorn kernels
watercress or parsley sprigs to garnish (optional)

■

Preparation time **40 minutes (less if using pre-cooked rice)**
Cooking time **15 minutes**
Oven temperature **180 C, 350 F, gas 4**

■

1 Have ready an ovenproof dish in which the tomatoes will sit comfortably.
2 Boil the rice in plenty of water for 25 minutes, or until cooked.
3 Cut the tops from the tomatoes and, using a serrated knife such as a grapefruit knife, remove the seeds and pulp. Reserve these in a bowl.
4 Stir the cooked, drained rice into the tomato pulp and flake the drained tuna into it.
5 Drain the sweetcorn and add this to the mixture. Mix well and pack into the tomato shells. Replace the lids and bake, covered, for 15 minutes. Garnish, if liked, with sprigs of watercress or parsley before serving.

It is a good idea to make this dish when you have some leftover cooked rice as this is a small amount to cook specially.

Tuna Tomatoes	
Per portion:	
Calories 140	
Fat 1g	
Fibre 4g	

Prawn Paella	
Per portion:	
Calories 320	
Fat 9g	
Fibre 6g	

Fish Soup

Per portion:
Calories 300
Fat 4g
Fibre 1g

FISH SOUP

SERVES 4

*1 tablespoon olive oil
1 large onion or 8 shallots, diced
2 cloves garlic, crushed
1 red or green pepper, deseeded and
diced
1 leek, sliced
175 g/6 oz prepared squid
1 grey mullet, about 350 g/12 oz
1 red mullet, about 225 g/8 oz
1 whiting, about 350 g/12 oz
1 litre/1½ pints vegetable or fish stock
sea salt
freshly ground black pepper
450 g/1 lb mussels*

■

Preparation time **30 minutes**
**(depending on whether you prepare
the fish yourself)**
Cooking time **30 minutes**

■

1 Heat the oil in a large saucepan and fry the onion, garlic, pepper and leek for 5 minutes, until soft but not brown.
2 Wash and slice the squid, if this has not been done by the fishmonger. Add to the vegetables.
3 Ask your fishmonger to gut and fillet the fish for you. If you wish to do this yourself, first descale the fish by running the blunt edge of a knife from tail to head – best done at the sink or over the waste bin. Gut the fish and remove the heads. Fillet and remove the skin before dicing the flesh.
4 Add the prepared fish and stock to the pan, cover, bring to the boil and simmer for 20 minutes. Season to taste.
5 Scrape the mussel shells, removing the barnacles and tugging off the 'beards'. Scrub with a brush under cold running water. Tap any open mussel sharply and discard any which do not close.
6 For the last 10 minutes of cooking, place the mussels on the top of the soup. Again, discard any mussels which have not opened during cooking.

You can never really achieve the genuine flavour of a Mediterranean bouillabaisse or fish soup which relies on fresh fish such as John Dory, rascasse and crayfish, but you can get the mullet in Britain relatively easily and you can use whiting and other fish for a good flavoured soup-come-stew. Try also monkfish, if available, and experiment with your own herb flavourings.

Garlic Toast

This makes a delicious accompaniment to this Mediterranean-style fish soup. Crush a clove of garlic and mix well with some unsalted butter. Toast some pieces of wholemeal bread on one side only and spread the untoasted side with the garlic butter. Place, butter side up, under the grill until golden. Serve at once and use to soak up the juices from the dish.

Fish Soup; Potato and Haddock Shells

POTATO AND HADDOCK SHELLS

MAKES 6

*350 g/12 oz potatoes
4½ tablespoons skimmed milk
350 g/12 oz smoked haddock fillet
1 onion, diced
1 green pepper, deseeded and diced
1 tablespoon vegetable oil
1 (142-g/5-oz) can sweetcorn kernels
1 tablespoon finely chopped parsley to garnish*

■

*Preparation time **40 minutes**
Cooking time **15 minutes**
Oven temperature **180 C, 350 F, gas 4**
(optional)*

■

1 Scrub the potatoes and peel, if liked.

Boil for 15–20 minutes until soft. Roughly mash them and place in a food processor or liquidiser with the milk and blend until smooth.
2 Spoon into a piping bag fitted with a 1-cm/½-in star nozzle and pipe a decorative edging around each scallop shell.
3 Poach the fish in just enough water to cover for 8–10 minutes, drain and – when cool enough to handle – flake the flesh from the skin and bones.
4 Sauté the onion and pepper in the oil until the onion is soft and transparent, but not browned.
5 Add the fish to the onion mixture and stir in the drained sweetcorn. Heat through, then pile into the centre of the shells and place under a moderate grill to warm through or place in the oven for about 15 minutes.
6 Garnish with the fresh parsley.

A delicious starter which freezes well. Serve in real or ceramic scallop shells.

Potato and Haddock Shells

Per shell:

Calories	160
Fat	3g
Fibre	3g

Salmon Terrine

Salmon Terrine
Per portion:
Serves 4:
Calories 170
Fat 10g
Fibre 1g
Serves 5:
Calories 135
Fat 8g
Fibre 1g
Serves 6:
Calories 110
Fat 7g
Fibre 1g

SALMON TERRINE

SERVES 4–6

225 g / 8 oz cold, cooked salmon
2 hard-boiled free-range eggs
2 teaspoons whole green peppercorns
1 red pepper, finely diced
4 shallots, finely diced
2 tablespoons chopped parsley
100 g / 4 oz button mushrooms, sliced
halved lemon slices and dill sprigs to garnish (optional)
Bouillon
600 ml / 1 pint water
1 bay leaf
1 small onion, quartered
1 carrot, quartered
green trimmings from a leek
½ lemon
6 black peppercorns
25 g / 1 oz powdered gelatine

■

*Preparation and cooking time **1 hour***

1 First prepare the bouillon. Place all the ingredients, except the gelatine, in a large saucepan. Bring to the boil and simmer for 20 minutes.

2 Strain the bouillon through a sieve lined with muslin. Sprinkle the gelatine over the hot liquid, stir until dissolved and leave until cool and syrupy.

3 Remove any skin and bones from the salmon and dice or flake the flesh.

4 Separate the egg yolks from the white and chop finely. Mix half the salmon with the yolk and half with the white.

5 When the bouillon and gelatine mixture is on the point of setting, place a thin layer of it in the base of a terrine dish. Mix together the remaining ingredients and place a third of the mixture in the terrine. Pour over a layer of bouillon. Place in the refrigerator or freezer to set.

6 Place a layer of fish and egg yolk on top of the set layer and pour over another layer of bouillon. Repeat with a layer of vegetables and bouillon, then the salmon and egg white. Finish with the vegetables.

7 Chill for 1 hour before turning out and

serving in slices. Garnish, if liked, with halved slices of lemon and sprigs of dill. *This dish does take a little time and trouble to prepare, but it is worth the effort. It is attractive and makes a little salmon go quite a long way.*

SEA BASS WITH TOMATO SAUCE

SERVES 4

*4 sea bass steaks
1 large onion, diced
1 red pepper, diced
1 tablespoon olive oil
1 (397-g/14-oz) can tomatoes
freshly ground black pepper
pinch of freshly grated nutmeg
300 ml/½ pint vegetable stock
sprig of thyme
thyme sprigs to garnish*

Preparation time **10 minutes**
Cooking time **25–30 minutes**
Oven temperature **180 C, 350 F, gas 4**

■

1 Place the fish in an ovenproof dish.
2 Place the onion and pepper in a pan with the oil and cook over a moderate heat for 5 minutes. Add the tomatoes and break them up well with the back of a wooden spoon.
3 Add the seasoning, stock and the leaves of thyme plucked from the sprig.
4 Cover the fish with this tomato sauce and cook for 25–30 minutes. Serve garnished with sprigs of thyme.

This recipe is based on the Mediterranean way of cooking chunky, close-textured fish such as sea bass and tuna in a tomato sauce flavoured with fresh thyme. If these fish are unavailable use a cod or coley steak, or monkfish if you are feeling a little more extravagant. Serve with brown rice or a salad. On its own it makes quite a satisfying light meal.

Sea Bass with Tomato Sauce	
Per portion:	
Calories 200	
Fat 4g	
Fibre 2g	

Sea Bass with Tomato Sauce

Smoked Mackerel Dip

Whole recipe:

Calories	360
Fat	17g
Fibre	0g

Smoked Haddock Tagliatelle

Per portion:

Calories	370
Fat	10g
Fibre	3g

Smoked Mackerel Dip (below); Smoked Haddock Tagliatelle; Moules Marinière with Garlic Bread

SMOKED MACKEREL DIP

SERVES 4

*2 smoked mackerel fillets
150 ml/¼ pint natural yogurt
2 blades mace
juice of ½ lemon
freshly ground black pepper
extra mace, lemon slices or parsley or
dill sprigs to garnish*

■

*Preparation time **5 minutes***

■

1 Skin the mackerel and pound the flesh or place in a food processor or liquidiser. Add the yogurt and purée until smooth.
2 Place the mace in a mortar and pound to a powder. Add to the fish and yogurt together with the lemon juice and pepper to taste. Chill before serving.
3 Garnish with a sprinkling of mace and with some slices of lemon or fresh herbs.

SMOKED HADDOCK TAGLIATELLE

SERVES 4

*450 g/1 lb smoked haddock fillet
225 g/8 oz courgettes
1 leek
1 green pepper
1 tablespoon corn oil
25 g/1 oz wholemeal flour
25 g/1 oz soft vegetable margarine
300 ml/½ pint skimmed milk
150 ml/¼ pint strained natural yogurt
freshly ground black pepper
225 g/8 oz fresh or 100 g/4 oz dried
green tagliatelle
2 tablespoons chopped fresh parsley*

■

*Preparation and cooking time **30 minutes***

■

1 Place the haddock in a large saucepan

and cover with water. Poach for 15 minutes, until cooked. Drain and – when cool enough to handle – remove the skin and bones and flake the flesh.

2 Blanch the courgettes for 1–2 minutes, drain and slice.

3 Slice the leek and deseed and dice the pepper. Sauté in the oil for 5 minutes.

4 Place the flour and margarine in another saucepan and stir over a moderate heat for a few minutes. Gradually add the milk, stirring between additions, to make a smooth sauce.

5 Remove from the heat and stir in the yogurt. Add the fish, courgettes and sautéd vegetables. Season with pepper.

6 Boil the pasta for 3 minutes, if fresh, or 10 minutes if dried. Drain and either place in a serving dish and top with the sauce and sprinkle with parsley or toss together the pasta and sauce with the parsley.

This creamy haddock sauce goes well with the green tagliatelle and this delicious combination makes a meal by itself. Add a salad if really hungry.

MOULES MARINIÈRE

SERVES 2

900 g / 2 lb fresh mussels
150 ml / ¼ pint dry white wine
2 cloves garlic, crushed
4 shallots, finely diced
2 tablespoons chopped parsley
parsley sprigs and lemon wedge to garnish
Garlic Bread
2 cloves garlic
40 g / 1½ oz unsalted butter
1 small, wholemeal French stick

■

Preparation time **30 minutes**
Cooking time **7 minutes**

■

1 Scrape the mussel shells well to remove any barnacles and pull off the 'beards'. Scrub the shells under cold running water. Tap any open mussels sharply and discard any which do not close.

2 Place the wine in a large saucepan and add one of the crushed garlic cloves and half the shallots.

3 Add the mussels to the pan and sprinkle over the remaining garlic and shallots and half the parsley.

4 Bring the wine to the boil, cover and cook the mussels for about 7 minutes until they are all open and heated through. Discard any mussels which do not open.

5 While the mussels are cooking, prepare the garlic bread. Crush the garlic and mash with the butter.

6 Cut the loaf in half lengthways or into slices and spread with the garlic butter. Place in the oven, or place each piece of the buttered bread, butter side up, under a hot grill so that the butter sinks in and the bread becomes brown and crisp.

7 Serve at once, sprinkling the remainder of the parsley over the mussels before serving. Garnish the dish with a sprig or two of parsley and a wedge of lemon.

Moules Marinière

Per portion:
Calories 180
Fat 8g
Fibre 0g

Stuffed Plaice

Stuffed Plaice	
Per portion:	
Calories	200
Fat	5g
Fibre	1g

STUFFED PLAICE

SERVES 6

6 large plaice fillets, black skin
removed
75g/3oz smoked cod's roe
50g/2oz wholemeal breadcrumbs
juice of 1 lemon
150ml/¼ pint strained natural yogurt
freshly ground black pepper
300ml/½ pint fish or vegetable stock

■

Preparation time **12–15 minutes**
Cooking time **25 minutes**
Oven temperature **180C, 350F, gas 4**

■

1 Have ready an ovenproof dish large
enough to take the fillets folded in half
and kept flat.
2 Wash the fish and leave to drain.
3 Skin the cod's roe and place in a food
processor or liquidiser. Add the
breadcrumbs, lemon juice, yogurt and
pepper and blend until smooth.
4 Place the fish flat on a work surface and
spread even amounts over one half of
each fillet. Fold the other half over the top

and transfer to the prepared dish.
5 Pour over the stock and bake in the
oven for 25 minutes, basting occasionally.

*Stuffing the plaice with a home-made
taramasalata mixture makes it a very
special meal. If you like, you could add a
tablespoon of concentrated tomato
purée to the cod's roe mixture for more
colour and flavour. Serve with new potatoes or brown rice and a green vegetable.
The taramasalata may also be used on its
own as a dip or spread.*

PRAWN PANCAKE GALETTE

SERVES 6

1 quantity wholemeal pancakes
(page 14)
225g/8oz broccoli spears
50g/2oz soft vegetable margarine
50g/2oz wholemeal flour
300ml/½ pint skimmed milk
1 teaspoon wholegrain mustard
100g/4oz peeled cooked prawns
lemon twists and dill sprigs to garnish

■

Preparation time **15 minutes, plus time
to make pancakes**
Cooking time **25 minutes**

■

1 Make up the pancakes, cover and keep
warm.
2 Trim the broccoli and boil or steam for
5 minutes, until tender. Dice well.
3 Place the margarine and flour in a
saucepan and stir over a low heat for a few
minutes. Gradually add the milk, stirring
between additions to prevent lumps
forming.
4 Remove from the heat and stir in the
mustard, the prawns and diced broccoli.
5 Place a pancake on the base of a warm
serving dish and top with a little sauce.
Top with a pancake and repeat until all
the sauce and pancakes are used up. Serve
at once, cut into wedges and garnished
with a twist of lemon and sprig of dill.

Prawn Pancake Galette

Per portion:

Calories 200

Fat 9g

Fibre 3g

Prawn Pancake Galette

Smoked Trout Mousse

Per portion:	
Calories 210	
Fat 7g	
Fibre 0g	

Peanut Prawn Cocktail (below); Smoked Trout Mousse; Scallops and Wild Rice

SMOKED TROUT MOUSSE

SERVES 4

275 g / 10 oz smoked trout
225 g / 8 oz low-fat soft cheese such as quark
juice of ½ lemon
50 g / 2 oz onion, grated
225 g / 8 oz strained natural yogurt
freshly ground black pepper
15 g / ½ oz powdered gelatine
4 tablespoons boiling water
2 free-range egg whites
chopped fresh herbs or ground mace to garnish

■

*Preparation time **20–25 minutes***
*Cooking time **1 hour***

■

1 Have ready four ramekins in which the mousse will be served.

2 Remove the skin and bones from the fish and flake finely.
3 Mash the fish with the cheese, lemon juice, onion, yogurt and pepper.
4 Sprinkle the gelatine onto the boiling water in a small bowl and stir until dissolved. Mix carefully and thoroughly into the fish mixture.
5 Whisk the egg whites until they form stiff peaks and gently mix in 2 tablespoons to lighten the mixture, then fold in the remainder.
6 Spoon into the ramekins and smooth the top. Chill for at least 1 hour before serving.
7 Garnish with fresh herbs or a little finely ground mace.

SCALLOPS AND WILD RICE

SERVES 2–4

75 g | 3 oz wild rice, washed
50 g | 2 oz shallots
50 g | 2 oz white leek
150 ml | ¼ pint white wine
1 bay leaf · 225 g | 8 oz scallops
pinch of saffron strands
6 green cardamoms
small knob unsalted butter
100 g | 4 oz peeled cooked prawns
Garnish (optional)
whole, unpeeled prawn
lemon twist · dill sprig

■

Preparation time **15 minutes**
Cooking time **25 minutes**

■

1 Boil the wild rice in plenty of water for 25 minutes, until cooked, then drain.

2 Dice the shallots and the leek and place in a saucepan with the wine and bay leaf and simmer for 10 minutes.
3 Slice the scallops.
4 Place the saffron strands and the seeds from the cardamom pods in a mortar and grind to a powder with a pestle.
5 Place the butter in a heavy-based pan and add the spices. Heat, then add the prepared scallops and prawns and cook through for 3–4 minutes.
6 Drain the leek mixture and mix with the shellfish in the pan, cook through for a further minute.
7 Place the fish in the centre of the scallop shells and arrange the rice around the outside. Garnish the plate with a whole prawn, twist of lemon and sprig of dill, if liked.

PEANUT PRAWN COCKTAIL

SERVES 4

3 shallots
1 large, ripe tomato, chopped
2 teaspoons olive oil
5 tablespoons vegetable or chicken stock
2 tablespoons peanut butter
100 g | 4 oz peeled cooked prawns
To serve
½ lettuce
thin slices brown bread and butter
lemon wedges

■

Preparation time **20 minutes**
Cooling time, if served cold **1½ hours**

■

1 Dice the shallots and place in a saucepan with the chopped tomato and oil and cook, covered, for 10 minutes.
2 Add the stock and stir in the peanut butter. Continue stirring to make a smooth paste.
3 Add the prawns and stir gently until heated through. Serve either hot or cold on a bed of lettuce leaves with slices of brown bread and butter. Offer lemon wedges separately.

Scallops and Wild Rice	
Per portion:	
Starter:	
Calories 200	
Fat 1g	
Fibre 1g	
Main course:	
Calories 400	
Fat 3g	
Fibre 3g	

Peanut Prawn Cocktail	
Per portion:	
Calories 100	
Fat 7g	
Fibre 1g	

POULTRY, GAME AND LAMB

This may seem a strange mixture, but the common denominator which brings them together is their suitability for people who enjoy meat but want to eat a wholefood diet and cut down on the amount of fat in their diet.

Poultry is the best known of the white meats that are low in fat. If you remove the skin from the chicken, you are removing the fattiest part of the bird and making it even better. If you buy free-range poultry the birds are less likely to contain drug residues, as well as having been humanely reared. These, and corn fed birds, are also unlikely to have been fed foods with additives.

Free-range poultry also shares with game the advantage of more of its fat being polyunsaturated than that of birds and other animals reared under intensive, 'sedentary' conditions. Game is also unlikely to have received any drug treatments. Lamb is another animal that lives a more 'natural' life and is allowed to exercise, producing more polyunsaturated fats (although it is still a fatty meat).

Organically produced meat is becoming more widely available as the demand for it grows.

Pigeon in Cabbage Leaves

PIGEON IN CABBAGE LEAVES

SERVES 4

2 pigeons, about 250g/9oz each
3 shallots, chopped
75g/3oz mushrooms, sliced
1 large carrot, diced
75g/3oz parsnip, diced
1 tablespoon oil
sea salt
freshly ground black pepper
1 teaspoon wholegrain mustard
8 large green cabbage leaves
Stock
6 parsley stalks
6 black peppercorns
2 bay leaves
1 carrot, quartered
cold water

*Preparation time **50 minutes***
*Cooking time **30 minutes***
*Oven temperature **190C, 375F, gas 5***

■

1 Lightly grease a 17-cm/7-in round ovenproof dish.

2 Roast the pigeons on a rack in a roasting pan, without additional fat, for 20 minutes. When cold enough to handle, remove and dice the flesh.

3 Now make a stock with the carcases. This can be used in the dish and also as gravy. Or you might like to use it for a soup as well (see note). Place the carcases in a saucepan with the parsley stalks, peppercorns, bay leaves and carrot. Cover with cold water. Bring to the boil and simmer for 15 minutes, then strain. Skim any fat off the top of the stock after it has stood for a while.

4 Place the shallots, mushrooms, carrot and parsnip in a saucepan with the oil and cover. Sauté for 5 minutes before seasoning with salt, pepper and mustard. Stir in the prepared meat.

5 Blanch the cabbage leaves in boiling water and drain. Line the prepared dish with them and spoon the meat mixture into the dish.

6 Pour in 150ml/$\frac{1}{4}$ pint of the prepared pigeon stock.

7 Fold the edges of the leaves over to seal and place some of the leaves on top to completely enclose the meat in a 'pie'. Bake for 30 minutes.

8 Pour off the excess gravy that will have been produced during cooking into a warmed jug. Unmould the pie onto a hot serving plate. Cut slices and serve with mashed potato and the reserved gravy, handed separately.

This is based on a delicious, but rather rich, course to a meal I had at the delightful El Amparo restaurant, Callejon de Puigcerda, Madrid. There the cabbage darioles were stuffed with smoked pigeon in a very rich mixture – here the dish is much lighter and made as one large 'pie' from which slices are cut.

Pigeon in Cabbage Leaves

Per portion:

Calories 180

Fat 11g

Fibre 2g

Why not make a pigeon soup with the remainder of the stock? Add to it a diced carrot, 2 sliced sticks of celery and 2 diced, unpeeled potatoes. Simmer for 15 minutes, then remove the celery and carrot and reserve. Purée the stock and potato in a food processor or liquidiser then return the celery and carrot and reheat. Adjust the seasoning and serve.

Chicken Croissants

Per croissant:

Calories	230
Fat	9g
Fibre	4g

Lamb Kebabs

Per portion:

Calories	200
Fat	10g
Fibre	2g

CHICKEN CROISSANTS

MAKES 6

225 g/8 oz wholemeal flour
50 g/2 oz soft vegetable margarine
15 g/½ oz fresh yeast
150 ml/¼ pint lukewarm water
beaten egg or milk to glaze
Filling
2 boneless chicken breasts, each
100–150 g/4–5 oz, skinned
juice of ½ lemon
100 g/4 oz mushrooms
2 tablespoons water
freshly ground black pepper
1 tablespoon chopped parsley

■

Preparation time **20 minutes**
Cooking time **25–30 minutes**
Oven temperature **200 C, 400 F, gas 6**

■

1 Sift the flour into a mixing bowl, returning the bran from the sieve to the flour, and add the fat. Rub in until the mixture resembles fine breadcrumbs.
2 Crumble the yeast into the water and mix well, then pour into the flour and mix to a dough. Knead lightly for 5 minutes.
3 Cover the dough and leave to rest in a warm place while you prepare the filling.
4 Grill the chicken breasts for 7 minutes each side, or until cooked through, basting with the lemon juice to prevent them drying out. When cool enough to handle, finely dice the flesh.
5 Wipe the mushrooms and slice if they are large, leave whole if they are the small, button type. Place the mushrooms in a saucepan with the water and cover. Cook gently for 5 minutes, then drain. Add the chicken and season with pepper.
6 Lightly grease a baking tray.
7 Roll out the pastry on a floured surface into a large circle of about 35 cm/14 in and score it to divide the circle into six segments.
8 Place some of the chicken and mushroom mixture around the outside of the circle. Sprinkle over the parsley and cut

through where you scored the dough.
9 Roll up the croissants from the outside edge to the centre of the circle and curve round into the traditional crescent shape. Glaze with lightly beaten egg or milk and place on the prepared tray. Bake for 25–30 minutes. Serve hot or cold.

Croissants are usually a very fatty, sweet, breakfast food. This is a savoury wholemeal version. The croissants are low in fat and filled with a low-calorie chicken and mushroom mixture to make an 'anytime' snack or meal. Serve on their own, or with a salad.

LAMB KEBABS

SERVES 4

450 g/1 lb lamb fillet
1 green pepper
1 red pepper
2 courgettes
2 small onions
100 g/4 oz button mushrooms
juice of 1 lemon for basting (optional)
Marinade (optional)
300 ml/½ pint red wine
2 cloves garlic, crushed

■

Preparation time **20–25 minutes, plus 12 hours to marinate (optional)**
Cooking time **15 minutes**

■

1 If barbecuing, remember to prepare the coals and start the fire well in advance so the barbecue is hot when you are ready to cook the kebabs.
2 Cut the lamb into bite-sized cubes. Using fillet of lamb should mean that there will be no waste of fat or bone, but trim off any fat as necessary. If marinating, place the meat in a dish when it has been trimmed and cover with the wine and garlic. Leave to stand, covered, in the refrigerator for 12 hours.
3 Prepare the other ingredients. Deseed the peppers and trim the ends off the courgettes, then cut into bite-sized pieces that will fit onto the skewers. Cut

*Chicken Croissants;
Lamb Kebabs*

Kebabs are a good way to cook meat because they allow any fat to drain away from the meat into the barbecue fire or grill pan. Baste the food with lemon juice, if necessary, to stop the vegetables drying out. If you blanch them first, they will cook more quickly and you will not be tempted to use any cooking oil.

the onions into eighths. Clean and trim the mushrooms. For quicker cooking, blanch the peppers, courgettes and onions for 1–2 minutes in boiling water, then drain.

4 Assemble the kebabs by arranging the items on the skewers in matching patterns.

5 To cook, place over the hot barbecue coals or under a moderate grill and turn frequently to avoid burning. Brush with lemon juice, if liked, to prevent the food drying out, but no oil is necessary.

Kebabs are delicious – especially cooked outdoors on a barbecue – but they can also be enjoyed inside. Marinating the lamb makes the meat cook more quickly but it is equally tasty without soaking in wine. Serve with a crisp green salad and warmed wholemeal pitta bread or on a bed of brown rice.

Leek-stuffed Chicken Breasts

Leek-stuffed Chicken Breasts	
Per portion:	
Calories 260	
Fat 11g	
Fibre 2g	

LEEK-STUFFED CHICKEN BREASTS

SERVES 2

15 g/½ oz unsalted butter
2 boneless chicken breasts, each about
150 g/5 oz, skinned
2 shallots · 100 g/4 oz leek
freshly ground black pepper

■

*Preparation time **15 minutes***
*Cooking time **12–15 minutes***
*Oven temperature **190 C, 375 F, gas 5***

■

1 Lightly grease an ovenproof dish.
2 Melt half the butter in a frying pan and lightly brown the chicken on both sides.
3 Dice the shallots finely and cut the leek into strips about 5-cm/2-in long. Place the shallots and leeks in a saucepan with the remaining butter. Cover and sweat gently for 5 minutes.
4 Take the chicken breasts from the pan and make a slit in them. Fill with the leek

mixture seasoned with the pepper.
5 Place in the prepared dish and pour over the cooking juices from the chicken pan and the leek pan.
6 Cover and bake for 12–15 minutes.

CHICKEN TERRINE

SERVES 4

75 g/3 oz whole green beans
75 g/3 oz carrots, cut into strips
2 boneless chicken breasts, skinned
200 g/7 oz quark or other low-fat, soft
white cheese
pinch of sea salt
freshly ground black pepper
¼ teaspoon chopped fresh thyme
2 free-range egg whites
thyme sprigs to garnish
Tomato Sauce
225 g/8 oz ripe tomatoes
2 tablespoons olive oil
2 tablespoons white wine vinegar
¼–½ teaspoon chopped fresh thyme
freshly ground black pepper

Chicken Terrine

*Preparation time **25 minutes***
*Cooking time **40 minutes, plus 2 hours
cooling time***
*Oven temperature **200 C, 400 F, gas 6***

■

1 Have ready a 900-g/2-lb loaf tin or terrine and a deep baking or roasting tin into which it will fit. (This will act as a water bath during cooking.)
2 Blanch the beans and carrots for 1–2 minutes in boiling water, then drain.
3 Mince the chicken breasts and beat in the cheese and salt and pepper to taste, then add the thyme.
4 Whisk the egg whites until stiff but not dry and fold into the mixture to make a chicken mousse.
5 Place one-third of the mousse in the base of the loaf tin or terrine and top with a layer of beans arranged in even rows running the length of the terrine. Top with half the remaining mousse mixture and repeat with the carrots. Top the whole dish with the rest of the mousse.
6 Place the loaf tin or terrine in the baking tin and fill the tin with boiling water.

7 Bake for 40 minutes.
8 While the terrine is cooking, make the sauce. Place the tomatoes in boiling water for 2 minutes, then drain and plunge into a bowl of cold water. Make a cut in the skins and peel the tomatoes. Place in a food processor or liquidiser and blend until smooth.
9 Strain the puréed tomatoes into a clean screwtop jar and add the oil, vinegar and thyme, then season to taste with pepper. Shake well.
10 When the terrine is cooked, remove from the oven and the baking dish and leave to cool for at least 2 hours. When cold, turn out and slice. Serve each slice in a pool of tomato sauce. Garnish the sliced terrine with a little fresh thyme.

This is really very simple to make and has an impressive appearance. It is also quite quick and a handy dish for summertime, either with salads or hot vegetables. The tomato sauce stores well in the refrigerator in a clean screwtop jar and can be used as an unusual salad dressing.

Chicken Terrine	
Per portion:	
Calories 210	
Fat 10g	
Fibre 2g	

Rabbit and Pheasant Sausages

Per sausage:

Calories 100

Fat 3g

Fibre 1g

Rabbit and Mustard in Cider

Per portion:

Calories 360

Fat 14g

Fibre 0g

RABBIT AND PHEASANT SAUSAGES

MAKES 10

225 g/8 oz boneless rabbit
225 g/8 oz boned pheasant or boneless chicken breast, skinned
1 onion
100 g/4 oz wholemeal breadcrumbs
150 ml/¼ pint vegetable or chicken stock
¼ teaspoon dried basil
¼ teaspoon dried tarragon
¼ teaspoon oregano
1 teaspoon wholegrain mustard

■

Preparation time **20 minutes**
Cooking time **20 minutes**
Oven temperature **180 C, 350 F, gas 4 (optional)**

■

1 Lightly grease a baking tray or have ready a non-stick one.
2 Mince the rabbit and the pheasant meat finely together using a mincer or a food processor.
3 Grate the onion very finely and mix this into the minced meat together with the breadcrumbs, stock, herbs and mustard.
4 The mixture should be firm, but pliable enough to mould into sausage shapes, and you will have enough to make 10 smallish sausages. They may appear smaller than standard sausages but they are much meatier and should not shrink so much during cooking as there is no fat to run away as they cook.
5 Cook under a grill or in the oven for 20 minutes, turning once if in the oven to ensure even browning. If grilling, use a low to moderate heat and turn several times.

Sausages are notoriously fatty and often made from poor quality meat or reconstituted meat slurry. They need the skins to hold together the fat and other ingredients, but these home-made game sausages are made from top quality, lean meat and are full of flavour without any additives! They have a coarser texture than regular sausages and can be made without all the bother of putting them into skins. One large rabbit leg and the breast of a meaty pheasant, plus other trimmings from the carcase (or two breasts) will supply all the meat needed.

RABBIT AND MUSTARD IN CIDER

SERVES 4

1 large rabbit or 4 rabbit joints
1 small jar Dijon mustard
1 large onion, diced
3 cloves garlic, crushed
2 sticks celery, finely sliced
1 tablespoon oil
600 ml/1 pint dry cider
150 ml/¼ pint natural yogurt

■

Preparation time **10 minutes, plus marinating time**
Cooking time **45 minutes**
Oven temperature **180 C, 350 F, gas 4**

■

1 Have ready an ovenproof dish in which the rabbit joints will fit.
2 If using a whole rabbit, joint it into leg joints and the saddle. Spread the portions generously with the mustard. At this stage they can be left in a cool place for several hours to marinate.
3 When ready to cook the dish, lightly sauté the onion, garlic and celery in the oil for 5 minutes, then add the rabbit and cook for a further 10 minutes.
4 Transfer to the ovenproof dish and pour over the cider. Cook for 30–35 minutes in the oven.
5 Remove from the oven and take the rabbit pieces from the liquid. Place on a serving dish and keep warm.
6 Place the liquid and vegetables in a food processor or liquidiser and blend to make

Rabbit and Pheasant Sausages (above); Rabbit and Mustard in Cider with Braised Greens

a smooth sauce. Return to the saucepan and heat through.

7 Remove from the heat and stir in the yogurt. Pour the sauce over the rabbit pieces and serve at once with the vegetables mentioned below.

Wild rabbit, if you can get it, gives a much better flavour to this dish than the farm-reared rabbit sold in most supermarkets and butchers.

Braised Greens

I like to serve this rabbit dish with shredded greens or kale with a sliced leek (allow 225 g/8 oz greens and I leek per person) sweated in a little unsalted butter. Sweat for 5 minutes, stirring to ensure the leeks do not burn or become too brown. Then leave to cook for a further 4–5 minutes over a low heat with the lid firmly on so that the vegetables cook in their own steam.

Braised Greens	
Per portion:	
Calories	100
Fat	6g
Fibre	11g

49

Goose with Apple and Ugli Fruit Sauce

Per portion:

Calories 700–870

Fat 30–50g

Fibre 8g

GOOSE WITH APPLE AND UGLI FRUIT SAUCE

SERVES 8

1 (2.25-kg/5-lb) goose
sage sprigs to garnish
Stuffing (optional)
50g/2oz celery
4 shallots
goose liver from the giblets
15g/½oz butter
225g/8oz sweet potato
1 cooking apple
1 tablespoon chopped fresh sage
freshly ground black pepper
100g/4oz wholemeal breadcrumbs
Stock and Gravy
giblets, minus the liver
1½ litres/3 pints water
4 shallots, halved
3 parsley stalks
sprig of thyme
8 peppercorns
1 celery stick, roughly chopped
Sauce
450g/1 lb cooking apples
6 tablespoons water
½ ugli fruit
15g/½oz unsalted butter

■

Preparation time **25 minutes**
Cooking time **2 hours**
Oven temperature **190 C, 375 F, gas 5**

■

Goose

1 Have ready a roasting tin with a rack which fits inside it on which the goose is to be placed.
2 Clean the goose and remove any of the yellow fat left inside the neck or main cavity.
3 Place the stuffing (if used) inside the goose and cook for 2 hours near the top of the oven. Protect the bird from over-browning or burning, if necessary, during the latter part of cooking by placing a double thickness of greaseproof paper or some aluminium foil loosely over the bird. Serve the goose in slices with the stuffing, if used, and sauce. Garnish each portion with a sage sprig and hand the gravy separately.

Stuffing

1 Finely dice the celery, shallots and liver and sauté them lightly in the butter.
2 Scrub the sweet potato and dice. Boil for 5 minutes to soften, then drain and add to the vegetable mixture.
3 Core and dice the apple and add to the mixture. Cook for a further 2–3 minutes. Stir in the sage and season with freshly ground black pepper.
4 If you like your stuffing smooth, blend it in a food processor or liquidiser. If you prefer a coarser texture, use the mixture as it is.
5 Finally add the breadcrumbs and use the mixture to stuff the goose.

Stock and Gravy

1 Place all the ingredients in a large saucepan and bring slowly to the boil.
2 Lower the heat and simmer for 30 minutes. Drain, discarding the vegetables, herbs and spices.
3 Use as much stock as required for gravy and retain the remainder for use in soups, casseroles etc.
4 To make gravy, add the cooking water of any vegetables you might be boiling to accompany the goose to the stock, then thicken with arrowroot, potato flour or a gravy mixture of your choice. Add some concentrated vegetable stock (such as Vecon) for extra flavour.

Sauce

1 Peel, core and slice the apples. Place in a saucepan with 4 tablespoons of the water and cook, covered, over a gentle heat for 5 minutes.
2 Peel and remove the segments from the ugli fruit, discarding any pips. Place in a saucepan with 2 tablespoons water and heat gently, breaking up the fruit.
3 Place the apple and ugli fruit in a food processor or liquidiser and blend until smooth. Return to a saucepan with the butter and simmer gently for a few minutes to reduce and thicken slightly.

The ugli fruit (a cross between an orange and grapefruit) here adds a delicious piquancy to the traditional apple sauce.

Goose with Apples and Ugli Fruit Sauce

Chicken Mousseline
Per portion:
Calories 340
Fat 19g
Fibre 4g

CHICKEN MOUSSELINE

SERVES 4

400 g | 14 oz boneless chicken breast, skinned
200 g | 7 oz quark or similar low-fat, soft white cheese
1 free-range egg yolk
10 fresh or bottled green peppercorns
1 teaspoon lemon juice
2 free-range egg whites
600 ml | 1 pint chicken or vegetable stock
675 g | 1½ lb tomatoes
4 tablespoons olive oil
2 tablespoons white wine vinegar
1 teaspoon prepared mustard
freshly ground black pepper
2 tablespoons snipped fresh chives
cherry tomatoes to garnish (optional)

■

Preparation time 20 minutes
Cooking time 20 minutes

■

1 Mince the chicken and beat in the cheese and egg yolk. Stir in the peppercorns and the lemon juice.
2 Whisk the egg whites until stiff but not dry and fold into the mixture.
3 Place half the stock in a large, shallow saucepan or frying pan and bring to simmering point.
4 Form small oval shapes of chicken mousseline between two dessertspoons and carefully drop into the liquid. Poach for 4 minutes each side. Remove and drain.
5 When you have cooked about 15, discard the stock and heat fresh stock to make the remaining mousselines.
6 Prepare the tomatoes by slicing thinly and tossing in vinaigrette made by placing the oil, vinegar, mustard and pepper in a clean screw-top jar and shaking vigorously to combine.
7 Place the tomatoes and dressing in a serving dish, sprinkle over the chives and top with the mousselines. Garnish with a few cherry tomatoes, if liked.

Pheasant with Sweet Potato and Aubergine
Per portion:
Calories 520
Fat 14g
Fibre 9g

PHEASANT WITH SWEET POTATO AND AUBERGINE

SERVES 2

1 (675-g | 1½-lb) pheasant
1 (225-g | 8-oz) sweet potato
1 (175-g | 6-oz) aubergine
100 g | 4 oz leek, chopped
1 Cox's dessert apple, cored and diced
4 tablespoons water
3 blades mace
1 teaspoon freshly grated nutmeg

■

Preparation time 20 minutes
Cooking time 40–45 minutes
Oven temperature 200 C, 400 F, gas 6

1 Soak the chicken brick according to the manufacturer's instructions.

2 Heat a heavy-based pan and brown the bird on all sides without using any fat. Discard any fat produced during browning.

3 Scrub the sweet potato and slice thickly into the bottom of the cooking brick.

4 Wash the aubergine and slice on top of the sweet potato.

5 Place the leek and apple in a saucepan with the water and sweat over a moderate heat for 5 minutes to soften.

6 Place the mace in a mortar and grind to a powder with the pestle. Add the nutmeg and stir into the leek and apple.

7 Spoon the mixture into the cavity of the bird and place it on top of the prepared vegetables.

8 Cook, covered, in the brick for 40–45 minutes.

The combination of sweet potato and slightly bitter aubergine makes an excellent base for the game and soaks up the juices from the bird during cooking. The leek and apple stuffing keeps the bird moist and cooking it in a chicken brick means that the pheasant does not have to be larded. The recipe, therefore, retains all the flavour and nutrients of the ingredients whilst keeping the dish moist and cutting down on fat. This dish is delicious served with Brussels sprouts.

Pheasant with Sweet Potato and Aubergine; Chicken Mousseline (above)

Boned, Stuffed Turkey

Boned, Stuffed Turkey	
Whole recipe:	
Calories	6400
Fat	325g
Fibre	60g

BONED, STUFFED TURKEY

SERVES ABOUT 25

1 (4-kg/9-lb) turkey, boned
celery leaves and parsley sprigs to garnish
Mushroom Stuffing
450g/1lb mushrooms, finely chopped
100g/4oz wholemeal breadcrumbs
2 onions, finely grated
1 leek, finely diced
175ml/6fl oz red wine
freshly ground black pepper
White Nut Stuffing
175g/6oz brazil nuts, ground
100g/4oz cashew nuts, ground
100g/4oz wholemeal breadcrumbs
1 free-range egg
25g/1oz fresh parsley, finely chopped
50g/2oz pistachio nuts
75g/3oz celery, sliced

*Preparation time **40 minutes***
*Cooking time **3¼ hours, plus 3 hours cooling time***
*Oven temperature **230C, 450F, gas 8***

■

1 To make the stuffings, mix each set of ingredients together to form a dough.
2 Place the turkey in a roasting tin and fill the cavity first with the mushroom stuffing, keeping a central cavity in which to place the white nut stuffing.
3 Form the white nut stuffing into a sausage shape and place in the centre.
4 Using a large trussing needle, sew up the bird.
5 Cook for 15 minutes and then, when the bird has browned, lower the heat to 180C, 350F, gas 4 and continue cooking for 3 hours.
6 Remove from the oven and drain off the juices, then leave to stand and become completely cold before carving into slices for serving. Garnish with celery leaves and sprigs of parsley.

A boned turkey makes carving easy and is a very impressive dish for special occasions. The two contrasting colours of stuffing add to the impressive effect. You will probably not want to bone the bird yourself, so ask your butcher a couple of weeks in advance to spare the time to prepare the bird for you.

DUCK BREASTS IN ORANGE SAUCE

SERVES 2

1 duck breast joint or 2 duck breasts
7 g / ¼ oz unsalted butter
watercress sprigs and orange slices to garnish
Sauce
50 g / 2 oz shallots, chopped
2 tomatoes, chopped
juice and ½ the grated rind of 1 orange
5 tablespoons dry white wine

Preparation time **20 minutes**
Cooking time **15–40 minutes**
Oven temperature **190 C, 375 F, gas 5**

■

1 Skin the duck breast joint or breasts. Lightly brown the duck in the butter.
2 While the duck is cooking, make the sauce. Place all the ingredients in a saucepan and simmer for 10 minutes. Liquidise and press through a sieve.
3 Place the browned duck breast in a heavy casserole and pour over the sauce.
4 If using a joint, cook for 40 minutes, if using 2 breasts, cook for 15–20 minutes. Serve garnished with sprigs of watercress and slices of orange.

A variation of the classic combination of duck and orange, this dish is much lower in fat than many traditional recipes and has a delightfully fresh tangy sauce. The fatty skin is discarded and only the lean meat is used.

The orange should yield 6 tablespoons of juice, make this quantity up with carton orange juice (or squeeze another!), if necessary.

Duck Breasts in Orange Sauce

Duck Breasts in Orange Sauce

Per portion:

Calories 250

Fat 5g

Fibre 2g

Indian Chicken in Yogurt Sauce

Per portion:	
Calories 90	
Fat 4g	
Fibre trace	

Indian Chicken in Yogurt Sauce; Potatoes with Coriander

It is often said that the British are conservative in their eating habits and certainly the traditional roast beef and Yorkshire pudding is far from extinct. Similarly, we are often accused of sticking persistently to prawn cocktail, steak and chips and Black Forest gâteau when 'eating out'.

But we have certainly incorporated many international foods in our diet. The popularity of takeaways confirms this where the ethnic restaurant competes favourably with the native fish and chip shop. Few high streets are without an Indian or Chinese takeaway, and American burger and rib restaurants are chasing the pizza restaurants in popularity.

However, most of these foods are high in fat and salt and, after a while, they become rather boring. We still like the taste of foreign foods so this section injects some more authentic foreign flavours in slightly more adventurous dishes. The recipes also use wholefood ingredients such as brown rice and yogurt and make the most of the cooking techniques that are lower in fat. Salt is also found unnecessary when using more exciting flavours from herbs and spices.

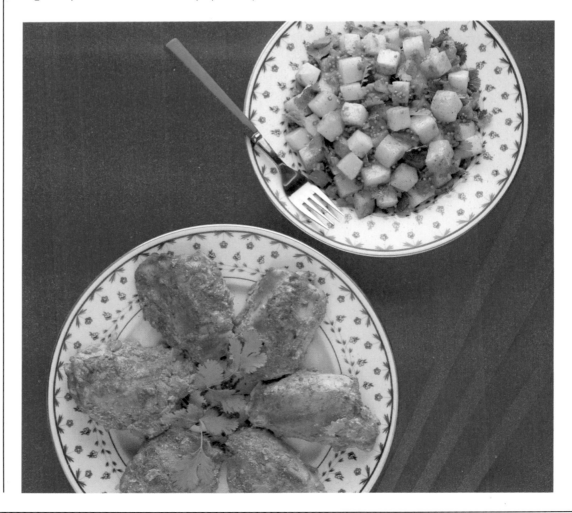

INDIAN CHICKEN IN YOGURT SAUCE

SERVES 6–8

1 (2.5-cm/1-in) piece fresh root ginger, grated
2 green chillies, deseeded and finely diced
2 cloves garlic, crushed
3 tablespoons natural yogurt
1 teaspoon cumin seeds, roasted and ground
pinch of sea salt
$\frac{1}{4}$ teaspoon turmeric
6–8 chicken thighs, skinned
2 teaspoons vegetable oil
1 large onion, diced
1 (227-g/8-oz) can tomatoes
$\frac{1}{2}$ teaspoon red chilli powder
4 cardamom seeds, ground (discard the pods)
$\frac{1}{2}$ teaspoon garam masala
coriander leaves to garnish (optional)

■

Preparation time **20 minutes, plus marinating time**
Cooking time **45–50 minutes**
Oven temperature **200 C, 400 F, gas 6**

■

1 Have ready a shallow, ovenproof dish.
2 Pound or grind together the ginger, chilli and garlic. Mix the yogurt, cumin seeds, salt and turmeric into the ground paste.
3 Coat the chicken with the paste and leave, covered, overnight or for several hours in the refrigerator.
4 Heat the oil in a heavy-based pan and add the onion. Cook until golden brown.
5 Add the tomatoes, breaking them up with the back of a spoon. Stir in the chilli powder, cardamom seeds and the garam masala.
6 Cook over a high heat to reduce the liquid for 10–15 minutes.
7 Add the chicken and marinade, mix and stir thoroughly. Transfer to the prepared dish and bake for 20 minutes near the top of the oven. Garnish the chicken with some coriander leaves, if liked.

This Indian chicken dish tastes good hot or cold and – despite the chillies and chilli powder – it is not, I think, too hot. Serve with Coriander Potatoes (below) for a delicious meal. It is worth buying the spices to make the dish properly. They keep for a long time and will encourage you to experiment with lots of new flavours for yourself.

POTATOES WITH CORIANDER

SERVES 8

450 g/1 lb potatoes
1 tablespoon vegetable oil
1 onion
225 g/8 oz tomatoes
2 teaspoons coriander seeds
1 teaspoon garam masala
1 tablespoon white mustard seeds
2 tablespoons fresh coriander leaves

■

Preparation time **15 minutes**
Cooking time **15 minutes**

■

1 Scrub the potatoes and dice into large cubes, but do not peel. Boil them for 5 minutes, then drain.
2 Place the oil in a saucepan over a low heat, add the potatoes and sauté gently for 5 minutes.
3 While the potatoes are cooking, dice the onion and finely chop the tomatoes. Add to the potatoes, together with the spices (except the coriander leaves).
4 Stir well to combine and continue to cook over a low heat with the lid on for a further 15 minutes, until the potatoes are just cooked. Be careful not to overcook or to mash the potatoes when stirring.
5 Remove from the heat and stir in the coriander leaves.

Diced potato in a thick tomato and coriander dressing.

Potatoes with Coriander

Per portion:

Calories 75

Fat 2g

Fibre 2g

You can buy fresh coriander in bunches, in the same way as you buy parsley, in Indian greengrocers and food stores. It is the Indian equivalent of parsley, but has large, flat leaves rather than the curled leaves of parsley and a different flavour. Cut the leaves from the stalk and use them whole to stir into, or garnish, dishes; or chop them finely as you do parsley.

Indian Black-eyed Beans

Per portion:

Calories	110
Fat	2g
Fibre	9g

Vegetable Pilau

Per portion:

Calories	125
Fat	2g
Fibre	2g

Brown rice should always be washed before use. The best way to do it is to place the rice in a bowl and cover well with water. Stir with the hand and all the chaff and dirt will rise to the surface and may be poured off. Repeat five times, or until the water is clean.

INDIAN BLACK-EYED BEANS

SERVES 8

225 g/8 oz black-eyed beans
50 g/2 oz okra
2 onions, diced
I green pepper, deseeded and diced
I tablespoon vegetable oil
I teaspoon cumin seeds
I tablespoon turmeric
2 (425-g/15-oz) cans tomatoes

■

*Preparation time **30 minutes, plus
soaking time for beans**
Cooking time **35 minutes***

■

I Wash the beans and soak them in boiling water overnight.
2 Next day boil for 30 minutes, then drain.
3 While the beans are cooking, wash the okra and dry well (they will become slimy if you add them to the mixture wet). Discard the stalks and tips and slice the rest of the okra into small rounds.
4 Place the okra, onion and pepper in a deep, heavy-based pan with the oil and spices. Cover and sweat for 10 minutes, stirring from time to time.
5 Add the tomatoes with their juice, breaking them up well with the back of a wooden spoon.
6 Add the beans, cover and simmer for a further 20–25 minutes.

VEGETABLE PILAU

SERVES 4

25 g/8 oz brown Basmati rice
4 dried red chillies
I vegetable stock cube
I tablespoon vegetable oil
½ teaspoon turmeric
50 g/2 oz okra
100 g/4 oz fresh or frozen peas
300 ml/½ pint vegetable stock

*Preparation and cooking time **45 minutes***

■

I Wash the rice in plenty of cold water and, when the water is clean, boil the rice with the chillies and stock cube in plenty of boiling water for about 20 minutes. Drain well.
2 Heat the oil in a large pan and add the turmeric. Stir in the drained rice and mix well to colour the rice.
3 Slice the okra into rounds, discarding the stalks and tips.
4 Add the vegetables and the stock and continue to cook for a further 10–15 minutes, until the moisture is absorbed.

Indian Black-eyed Beans;
Vegetable Pilau; Spinach
Dhal (above)

SPINACH DHAL

SERVES 4

225 g/8 oz whole green lentils
1 (2.5-cm/1-in) piece fresh root ginger
2 onions, chopped
2 cloves garlic, crushed
1 tablespoon corn oil
1 teaspoon each of turmeric, garam
masala, ground coriander and ground
cumin
½ teaspoon paprika
½ aubergine, sliced
2 tablespoons water
450 g/1 lb fresh spinach or Swiss chard,
washed and finely chopped
coriander leaves to garnish

Preparation time 15 minutes
Cooking time 40 minutes

■

1 Wash and pick over the lentils, then boil in plenty of water for 20 minutes.
2 Peel and grate the ginger and place with the onion and garlic in a heavy-based pan with the oil. Sauté gently for 5 minutes, stirring occasionally.
3 Sprinkle the spices over the top, then add the aubergine and water. Cover and cook over a low heat for a further 5 minutes.
4 Add the cooked lentils and spinach. Cover and cook for a further 10 minutes, adding a little more water if necessary. The mixture should not be wet or sloppy. Serve with boiled brown rice, garnished with a sprig of coriander leaves.

Spinach Dhal	
Per portion:	
Calories 240	
Fat 4g	
Fibre 12g	

**Sesame Chicken
(without skin)**

Per portion:

Calories 350

Fat 18g

Fibre 2g

Shoyu is the naturally fermented version of soy sauce. I use it because it is free from added monosodium glutamate. Some good quality soy sauce is also free from additives. Tamari is the Japanese natural soy sauce.

Sesame Chicken

SESAME CHICKEN

SERVES 4

1 (1.25-kg/2½-lb) chicken
40g/1½ oz sesame seeds
½ teaspoon sea salt · 1 teaspoon oil
watercress sprig to garnish (optional)
Vegetables
2 tablespoons sesame oil
1 (2.5-cm/1-in) piece fresh root ginger
2 cloves garlic, crushed
2 large carrots, cut into matchsticks
1 green pepper, deseeded and sliced into rounds
1 yellow pepper, deseeded and cut into strips
2 leeks, sliced into circles
1 (227-g/8-oz) can bamboo shoots
50g/2oz beansprouts
Sauce
5 tablespoons orange juice
1 tablespoon tomato ketchup
2 tablespoons shoyu sauce
2 tablespoons rice vinegar
1 tablespoon tamari
2 teaspoons demerara sugar
1 teaspoon arrowroot, potato flour or cornflour (optional)

*Preparation time **20 minutes***
*Cooking time **1 hour***
*Oven temperature **200 C, 400 F, gas 6***
■

1 Grind the sesame seeds with the salt using a pestle and mortar and then brush the chicken very lightly with some oil. Scatter the ground seeds over the bird and roast for 1 hour on a rack in a roasting tin.

2 Cook the vegetables just before the chicken is ready. Place the sesame oil in a wok or large frying pan. Finely grate the ginger and add with the garlic.

3 Heat the oil until hot but not smoking. Add the prepared vegetables in order and stir-fry for about 5 minutes. A minute or two before serving, add the beansprouts.

4 To make the sauce, simply place all the ingredients except the arrowroot in a saucepan and stir over a gentle heat until the sugar has melted. If you prefer a thicker sauce, it can be thickened by adding a little arrowroot, potato flour or cornflour slaked in water. Stir over the heat until thickened.

5 You can either pour the sweet and sour sauce over the vegetables just as they finish cooking and turn them in it for a

minute, or you can hand the sauce separately. Garnish with a sprig of watercress if liked.

Stir-frying vegetables is an excellent way of keeping them crisp and tasty. It also retains vitamins because of the short cooking time without the water in which nutrients are lost. They look very colourful and are an excellent, moist accompaniment to chicken roasted without added fat. Don't be put off by the long list of ingredients. This is very simple to make, and very tasty.

AFRICAN GROUNDNUT AND CHICKEN STEW

SERVES 4

*3 boneless chicken breasts, skinned
juice of 1 lemon
2 onions, diced
1 green chilli, deseeded and finely chopped
1 (1-cm/½-in) piece fresh root ginger, finely grated
1 tablespoon vegetable oil
1 (397-g/14-oz) can tomatoes
2 tablespoons peanut butter
1 aubergine
100g/4oz okra
coriander leaves to garnish (optional)*
To serve
*A selection from the following:
1 mango, 1 ripe banana, ½ pineapple, 1 orange, 1 pawpaw*

■

*Preparation and cooking time **45–50 minutes***

■

1 Grill the chicken under a moderate heat, basting with the lemon juice to prevent it drying out. When just cooked, shred or dice and place on one side.
2 Place the onion, chilli and ginger in a frying pan with the oil and sauté gently for 5 minutes without browning.

3 Stir in the tomatoes and their juices and break up the tomatoes with the back of a wooden spoon.
4 Add the peanut butter and the reserved chicken. Stir well and leave to cook over a very low heat.
5 Dice the aubergine and wash the okra and dry well. Trim off the stalks and tips, then slice. Steam or boil the aubergine and okra until just soft – about 10 minutes.
6 Drain the aubergine and okra and stir into the chicken stew. Serve at once with a mixture of freshly prepared, exotic chopped fruits such as those listed above and some plain, boiled brown rice. Garnish with coriander leaves, if liked.

An unusual, but delicious, combination of chicken in a thick and creamy sauce served with fresh fruit, African-style, rather than vegetables. You must try it!

African Groundnut and Chicken Stew

African Groundnut and Chicken Stew

Per portion:

Calories 500

Fat 35g

Fibre 8g

Szechuan Chilli Prawns

Szechuan Chilli Prawns	
Per portion:	
Calories 135	
Fat 5g	
Fibre 2g	

SZECHUAN CHILLI PRAWNS

SERVES 4

2 cloves garlic, crushed
2 onions, diced
3 green chillies, deseeded and diced
1 tablespoon olive oil
4 black cardamoms
$\frac{1}{2}$ teaspoon coriander seeds
$\frac{1}{2}$ teaspoon paprika
juice of 1 orange
1 (397-g/14-oz) can tomatoes
1 tablespoon concentrated tomato purée
225 g/8 oz peeled cooked prawns

Garnish
whole, cooked prawns
orange slices
watercress sprigs

*Preparation time **15 minutes**
Cooking time **20 minutes***

■

1 Place the garlic, onion and chilli in the oil and sauté over a low heat for 5 minutes to soften. Do not brown.
2 Meanwhile, remove the seeds from the cardamoms and crush, using a pestle and mortar, with the coriander seed. Add to the onion mixture with the paprika.
3 Stir well and continue cooking for a few minutes. Add the orange juice, the tomatoes with their juice and the tomato purée. Break up the tomatoes well using the back of a wooden spoon. Simmer for a further 10 minutes.
4 Stir in the prawns and cook gently for another 5 minutes until they are heated through. Serve hot with boiled rice and garnished with a couple of whole prawns, slices of orange and sprig of watercress.

Mexican Beans

MEXICAN BEANS

SERVES 4

225 g/8 oz dried red kidney beans,
soaked overnight
225 g/8 oz dried butter beans, soaked
overnight
1 large onion, diced
1 large green pepper, deseeded and
diced
2 cloves garlic, crushed
2 green chillies, deseeded and diced
1 tablespoon vegetable oil
1 teaspoon ground cumin
$\frac{1}{2}$ teaspoon ground coriander
2 (397-g/14-oz) cans tomatoes
225 g/8 oz long-grain brown rice
watercress sprig to garnish

■

Preparation time **20 minutes,
plus 1 hour for cooking beans**
Cooking time **35 minutes**

1 Place the soaked beans in separate pans and cover with cold water. Bring to the boil and boil hard for 10 minutes. Reduce the heat and simmer for 40–50 minutes.
2 Place the onion, pepper, garlic and chillies in a saucepan with the oil and sauté for 5 minutes, stirring from time to time until the onion is transparent.
3 Stir in the cumin, coriander and tomatoes, breaking them up with the back of a wooden spoon.
4 Add the drained beans, cover and simmer for 20 minutes.
5 Meanwhile, boil the washed rice in plenty of boiling water for about 35 minutes. Serve the beans on the rice, garnished with a sprig of watercress.

If you like the flavour of chilli con carne then you will like this vegetarian version based on beans. Like meat chilli, serve with brown rice or a baked potato.

Mexican Beans
Per portion:
Calories 580
Fat 5g
Fibre 32g

Hot Caribbean Soup

Per portion:
Calories 125
Fat 4g
Fibre 2g

HOT CARIBBEAN SOUP

SERVES 4

100 g/4 oz shallots, finely chopped
1 tablespoon olive oil
2 green chillies, deseeded and finely chopped
1 (2.5-cm/1-in) piece fresh root ginger, finely chopped
1 red pepper, deseeded and finely chopped
50 g/2 oz okra, sliced
225 g/8 oz white fish fillet
100 g/4 oz peeled cooked prawns
juice of 1 lime
$\frac{1}{4}$ teaspoon paprika
1 (397-g/14-oz) can tomatoes
$\frac{1}{2}$ vegetable stock cube
300 ml/$\frac{1}{2}$ pint boiling water
whole, cooked prawns and lime slices to garnish

■

*Preparation time **20 minutes***
*Cooking time **20 minutes***

■

1 Sauté the shallots in the oil in a large saucepan over a low heat.
2 Add the chillies, ginger, pepper and okra. Cover and cook gently for 5 minutes, stirring occasionally.
3 Cut the fish into cubes, removing any skin and bones.
4 Add the prawns and white fish to the pan and cook for a further 5 minutes.
5 Add the lime juice, paprika and the tomatoes, breaking them up with the back of a wooden spoon.
6 Dissolve the stock cube in the water and add to the pan. Cover and leave to simmer for 20 minutes. Serve hot garnished with prawns and slices of lime.

A hot, spicy fish soup inspired by the flavours and texture of Caribbean food. It is one of my favourites and a superb meal in itself with either a wholemeal roll, or crispbread. A cheap white fish such as coley may be used.

Escovitch Fish

Per portion:
Calories 240
Fat 2g
Fibre 3g

ESCOVITCH FISH

SERVES 4

4 small red mullet, gutted and cleaned
juice of 1 lemon
1$\frac{1}{2}$ tablespoons freshly ground black pepper
1 kg/2 lb small onions
2 Jamaican bell peppers or 3 green chillies
150 ml/$\frac{1}{4}$ pint white wine vinegar

■

*Preparation time **30 minutes***
*Cooking time **30 minutes, plus 1 hour marinating time***
*Oven temperature **170 C, 325 F, gas 3***

Hot Caribbean Soup;
Escovitch Fish

1 Have ready a deep, ovenproof dish.
2 Rub the fish with the lemon juice. Rub the pepper into the gut cavities.
3 Slice all but 2 onions into rings and place in the base of the dish, then lay the fish on top.
4 Bake for 30 minutes, covered, then remove the dish from the oven and place the fish on one side.
5 Discard the onions (saving them for soup or stock if liked) and cut the remaining onions into rings.
6 Slice the peppers or chillies, removing the seeds, and place the onion, peppers or chillies and vinegar in a pan. Bring to the boil and simmer for 5 minutes.
7 Remove from the heat and cool, then pour over the fish and leave to marinate

for at least 1 hour before serving.

This is a spicy Caribbean dish I discovered from a terrific team of girls who run a Caribbean catering company. The amount of pepper in it is right and the results are really spicy—but still delicious. If Jamaican bell peppers (from a West Indian grocer) are unavailable, use fresh green chillies. The fish is first cooked, then marinated before serving.

Turkish-style Partridge (above); Goan Chicken with Kumquats; Chinese Chicken Pancakes

Goan Chicken with Kumquats

Per portion:
Calories 170
Fat 5g
Fibre 1g

GOAN CHICKEN WITH KUMQUATS

SERVES 4

*1 (1.25-kg/2½-lb) chicken
100g/4oz kumquats
2 green chillies, deseeded and finely chopped
4 shallots, finely chopped
sea salt
freshly ground black pepper
2 teaspoons ground coriander
½ teaspoon turmeric
coriander leaves and kumquat slices to garnish*

■

*Preparation time **15–20 minutes, plus overnight marinating***
*Cooking time **about 1 hour***
*Oven temperature **200 C, 400 F, gas 6***

■

1 Clean the chicken and skin it, then place on a dish that will fit inside the refrigerator with the bird on it.
2 Scrub the kumquats and chop roughly.

Place in a food processor or liquidiser and blend to a purée, then pick out any pips or tough skin from the segments (you may prefer to do this before blending).
3 Mix together all the remaining ingredients with the kumquat purée to make the marinating paste.
4 Spread the paste evenly all over the skinned chicken and leave in the refrigerator to marinate overnight.
5 Roast the chicken with the paste for about 1 hour, until the juices run clear. Garnish this dish with a little fresh coriander and a few slices of kumquat.

This recipe is based on a traditional marinating paste from Goa in India. The kumquats make it deliciously spicy and aromatic. If you have not used kumquats before, they are like very small oranges with a slightly bitter flavour.

CHINESE CHICKEN PANCAKES

SERVES 4

*1 quantity wholemeal pancakes
(page 14)
2 boneless chicken breasts, skinned
1 tablespoon vegetable oil
1 clove garlic, crushed
1 onion, chopped
1 (2.5-cm/1-in) piece fresh root ginger,
grated
3 carrots, cut into matchsticks
100g/4oz beansprouts
coriander leaves and orange slices to
garnish (optional)*
Sauce
*2 tablespoons shoyu sauce
1 tablespoon red wine vinegar
grated rind and juice of 1 orange
2 teaspoons demerara sugar*

■

*Preparation time **10 minutes, plus
pancake preparation time***
*Cooking time **12–15 minutes***

1 Prepare the pancakes and keep warm.
2 Shred the chicken and stir-fry in the oil with the garlic, onion and ginger.
3 Cook for 5 minutes, stirring well, then add the carrots and continue to cook for a further 5 minutes.
4 Meanwhile, cook the sauce by placing all the ingredients in a saucepan and heating well. Pour over the chicken.
5 Add the beansprouts and cook for 1 minute. Place the filling in the pancakes, roll up and serve at once. If liked, you can garnish the stuffed pancakes with coriander leaves and halved slices of orange.

TURKISH-STYLE PARTRIDGE

SERVES 2

*100g/4oz brown rice
50g/2oz currants
1 teaspoon ground cinnamon
50g/2oz almonds, roasted
2 partridges
1 tablespoon olive oil
3 small parsnips, scrubbed
4 tablespoons boiling water
watercress sprigs to garnish*

■

*Preparation time **35 minutes***
*Cooking time **40–45 minutes***
*Oven temperature **190C, 375F, gas 5***

■

1 Boil the rice in plenty of water for 25–35 minutes, then drain.
2 Stir the currants and cinnamon into the rice. Roughly chop the nuts and stir in.
3 Brown the partridges all over in the oil.
4 Slice the parsnips into about four strips, lengthways, and brown in the oil remaining in the frying pan from browning the partridges.
5 Place the rice in a marmite or heavy casserole and add the boiling water.
6 Place the browned partridges on top. Cover with the browned parsnips, cover with a lid and cook for 40–45 minutes. Place on a serving dish and garnish with a few sprigs of watercress.

Chinese Chicken Pancakes

Per portion:	
Calories 265	
Fat 8g	
Fibre 5g	

Turkish-style Partridge

Per portion:	
Calories 800	
Fat 30g	
Fibre 12g	

DESSERTS

A healthy diet is the result of the sum total of our food and, so long as we achieve the broad goals laid down by experts (and outlined in *Creative Wholefoods*), we should not worry about every mouthful.

Cutting down on the number of puddings we eat each day will help meet these goals, especially in terms of fat and sugar. We would do well to limit pudding to one meal a day and certainly fewer puds would be better, finishing the meal with a piece of fresh fruit instead.

There are also changes we can make to the type of puddings we enjoy. This does not mean leaving soufflés, crêpes, gâteaux and cheesecakes off the menu, but altering the basic ingredients from which they are made. For example, strained yogurt can be substituted for cream, whether it is used as an accompaniment or in recipes, and we can use more fruit-based desserts. We can also find alternative sweeteners to sugar and make other subtle changes to the ingredients, such as those you will find in this section, to produce recipes that make a lot of nutritional sense and, just as importantly, taste good.

Guava Cheesecake

GUAVA CHEESECAKE

SERVES 8

4 guavas
75 g / 3 oz soft vegetable margarine
225 g / 8 oz digestive biscuits
15 g / ½ oz powdered gelatine
4 tablespoons boiling water
175 g / 6 oz quark or other low-fat
soft cheese
250 ml / 8 fl oz strained natural yogurt
175 g / 6 oz no-added sugar black
cherry jam
guava slices and mint or lemon balm
sprig to decorate (optional)

Preparation time **20 minutes**
Cooking time **1 hour**

■

1 Peel the guavas and quarter the fruit, but do not bother to remove the pips. Poach in a little water for 15 minutes.

2 Drain, reserving the liquid for a fruit salad, or compote. Cool slightly and purée the fruit in a food processor or liquidiser. Sieve to remove the pips, remembering to collect all the pulp from the base of the sieve.

3 Melt the margarine in a saucepan while the guavas are cooking and crush the biscuits to crumbs. Stir together and press into the base of a 20-cm / 8-in loose-bottomed cake or deep flan tin. Place in the refrigerator to chill.

4 Sprinkle the gelatine on top of the boiling water and stir to dissolve. Leave on one side.

5 Place the cooled guava purée in a mixing bowl with the quark and yogurt and mix well. Stir in the gelatine, mixing thoroughly, and pour on top of the prepared base. Return the cheesecake to the refrigerator.

6 When the cheesecake has set, place the jam in a saucepan and heat until runny, then spoon over the top of the cheesecake to make an attractive topping.

7 Return to the refrigerator and chill before serving. This cheesecake also freezes well. Freshly sliced guavas can be used for decoration, if desired, with a sprig of mint or lemon balm for extra interest.

Guavas are highly scented with an aromatic sweet taste. They make excellent purées which are ideal for cheesecakes or as a pancake filling. The scent will fill the whole kitchen, especially if they are left out on a worktop in a warm room. Guavas have a thin green skin which turns light yellow when ripe, rather like a shiny pear skin. The flesh varies from white to yellow and deep pink. The hard pips are sieved out in this recipe, but they are edible.

Guava Cheesecake	
Per portion:	
Calories 320	
Fat 15g	
Fibre 4g	

A fresh fruit jelly is a good way of introducing a dessert free from added sugar and fats to your family. Of course the fruits can be varied according to the season.

Mango Fruit Terrine	
Per portion:	
Calories	75
Fat	0g
Fibre	2g

MANGO FRUIT TERRINE

SERVES 8

1 (200-ml/7-fl oz) carton Marks and Spencer mango and apple juice or orange juice
15 g/½ oz powdered gelatine
150 ml/¼ pint boiling water
½ red-skinned dessert apple
2 small bananas
1 pink grapefruit
1 mango
2 small, ripe pears
100 g/4 oz strawberries
fresh mint leaves to decorate (optional)

■

Preparation time **30 minutes**
Cooking time **1 hour**

■

1 Place the juice in a jug or basin.
2 Sprinkle the gelatine onto the boiling water and stir until dissolved. Stir into the juice and put in the refrigerator to cool and start to set.
3 Wash and core the apple, but do not peel. Dice finely into a bowl.
4 Slice the bananas and add to the apple.
5 Peel the grapefruit and cut into segments, removing any pith and membranes.
6 Peel and slice the mango.
7 Peel, core and dice the pears.
8 Pick over and hull the strawberries. Halve if large and reserve eight for decoration.
9 Mix together all the fruit and place in a loaf tin, terrine or fancy-shaped mould. Pour over the mango and apple juice, which will be on the point of setting, and pack the fruit down into the juice.
10 Chill in the refrigerator for 1 hour to set before serving.
11 To serve, either cut slices from the terrine or un-mould and slice. Place the slices on individual serving plates, topped with a strawberry. Alternatively, un-mould onto a large serving dish and garnish with sliced strawberries and, perhaps, some mint leaves

Mangoes are tipped to become one of the most popular of the exotic fruits in the 1980s and once you have tasted this recipe you will understand why. This real fruit jelly makes the most of their delicious flavour while combining them with other fruit to make them go further.

CHERRY CLAFOUTIS

SERVES 4

450 g/1 lb black cherries
2 free-range eggs
2 tablespoons wholemeal flour
300 ml/½ pint skimmed milk
1 tablespoon clear honey

■

Preparation time **20 minutes**
Cooking time **25–30 minutes**
Oven temperature **200 C, 400 F, gas 6**

■

1 Lightly butter an ovenproof dish.
2 Wash the cherries and remove the stalks. If using bottled or canned fruit, drain off the syrup or juice. (Choose fruit bottled in juice, or a light syrup.)
3 Beat the eggs and flour together in a basin.
4 Heat the milk until amost boiling, then pour onto the eggs, whisking well.
5 Place the cherries in the dish and pour over the batter. Drizzle over the honey and bake for 25–30 minutes.

This delicious French dessert can be made equally well with wholemeal flour. Serve at once when it is cooked – unfortunately it does not keep.

Cherry Clafoutis

Per portion:

Calories 150

Fat 3g

Fibre 2g

Cherry Clafoutis;
Mango Fruit Terrine

**Prune and Brandy
Ice Cream**

Per portion:	
Calories 170	
Fat 7g	
Fibre 5g	

*Prune and Brandy Ice
Cream*

**This recipe can be
made by hand if you do
not have an ice cream
churn. Follow the
recipe as above but
instead of churning the
mixture, pour it into a
large polythene
container or bowl and
place in the freezer.
When the mixture
becomes slushy remove
from the freezer and
whisk well. Repeat this
procedure before
leaving the ice cream
to become hard. The
resulting ice cream will
be a little more 'grainy'
in texture but just as
delicious.**

PRUNE AND BRANDY ICE CREAM

SERVES 6

*225 g/8 oz prunes, soaked overnight if
necessary
300 ml/½ pint strained natural yogurt
3 tablespoons brandy
2 free-range egg whites
150 ml/¼ pint soured cream*

■

Preparation time **30 minutes**
Freezing time **2 hours**

■

I Cook the prunes in water until soft and
– when cool enough to handle – remove
the stones.

2 Place the stoned prunes in a food
processor or liquidiser with the yogurt
and brandy and blend until smooth.
3 Whisk the egg whites until stiff but not
dry.
4 Mix the soured cream into the prune
mixture then fold in the egg whites.
5 Pour into an ice-cream machine to
churn and, when stiff, turn into a container and freeze.
6 Remember to remove from the freezer
about 30 minutes before serving to allow
the flavour to develop and the ice cream
to become soft enough to serve.

*Ice creams are usually made with double
cream and egg yolks, or custard, but this
one makes use of low-fat yogurt and some
soured cream which is lower in calories
than double or whipping cream. This ice
cream is also free from added sugar,
deriving sweetness from the prunes. You
can accompany this dish with a few
biscuits, if liked.*

PUMPKIN PIE

SERVES 8

*450g/1 lb pumpkin
2 free-range eggs
½ teaspoon each of ground cinnamon,
freshly grated nutmeg and ground
allspice
¼ teaspoon ground cloves
1 tablespoon Muscovado sugar
300 ml/½ pint skimmed milk
1 tablespoon honey
strained natural yogurt to serve*
Pastry
*175g/6oz wholemeal flour
75g/3oz soft vegetable margarine
a little cold water*

■

Preparation time **20–25 minutes**
Cooking time **30 minutes**
Oven temperature **190C, 375F, gas 5**

■

1 Lightly grease a 20-cm/8-in flan dish or ceramic dish.
2 Peel the pumpkin and boil until just soft – about 15 minutes. Drain well.
3 While the pumpkin is cooking, make the pastry. Sift the flour, returning the bran from the sieve to the bowl, and rub the fat in until the mixture resembles fine breadcrumbs.
4 Bind with a little cold water to make a soft dough. Roll out the pastry and use to line the prepared flan tin.
5 Purée the cooked pumpkin in a food processor or liquidiser, or push through a nylon sieve.
6 Beat the eggs lightly with the spices and sugar. Bring the milk to almost boiling point in a saucepan. Remove from the heat and pour onto the egg mixture, whisking all the time. Mix with the pumpkin purée and pour into the prepared pastry case.
7 Drizzle over the honey and bake for 30 minutes. Allow to cool and set before serving slightly warm or cold with strained natural yogurt.

Pumpkin pie is a traditional American dessert that lends itself very well to a wholemeal pastry case. It is a deliciously spiced pumpkin custard with a glorious autumnal golden colour. This recipe is not as sugary and sweet as many other American favourites.

Pumpkin Pie	
Per portion:	
Calories 200	
Fat 9g	
Fibre 2g	

Pumpkin Pie with strained natural yogurt

Creative Apple Pie	
Per portion:	
Calories 340	
Fat 16g	
Fibre 6g	

Real Custard	
Per portion:	
Calories 270	
Fat 6g	
Fibre 0g	

Creative Apple Pie with Real Custard

CREATIVE APPLE PIE

SERVES 4

*I quantity wholemeal shortcrust pastry
(see Pumpkin Pie, page 73)
450 g/1 lb cooking apples
4 tablespoons water
50 g/2 oz dried peaches or pears
4 cloves
I teaspoon mixed spice
lightly beaten egg or milk to glaze*

■

*Preparation time **25 minutes**
Cooking time **30 minutes**
Oven temperature **200 C, 400 F, gas 6***

■

I Make the pastry.
2 Wash and core the apples, then slice into a saucepan with the water. Chop the peaches or pears and add to the apples, together with the cloves and mixed spice. Cover and cook over a low heat for 10 minutes.
3 Remove from the heat and allow to cool while you roll out the pastry and use to line a small pie dish, leaving enough pastry to make a lid for the pie.
4 Pour the fruit and its juice into the pie. Place the lid on top, sealing the edges with lightly beaten egg or milk. Glaze the top with the same and make a hole in the centre for the steam to escape. Bake for 30 minutes.
5 Serve with Real Custard (see below).

Apple pie might not seem to you 'creative' but just see what a difference is made by adding the dried peaches or pears and the cloves. Creative cooking is just as much about giving old favourites a new flavour and identity as it is about creating new dishes.

REAL CUSTARD

MAKES 300 ml/½ pint

*300 ml/½ pint skimmed milk
I free-range egg
I tablespoon light Muscavado sugar or
clear honey
3 drops natural vanilla essence*

■

I Bring the milk nearly to boiling point in a saucepan, then remove from the heat.
2 Beat the egg and sugar or honey together in a bowl and pour the milk onto this, whisking all the time.
3 Return to a clean pan (using the same one as you heated the milk in will risk it catching on the bottom and burning) and stir over a moderate heat until slightly thickened. Do not boil or the custard will curdle.
4 Stir in the vanilla essence, cook for a minute more and serve.

Apple pie would not be apple pie without custard. Make sure it's the real thing.

Strawberry and Pineapple Hazelnut Torte

STRAWBERRY AND PINEAPPLE HAZELNUT TORTE

SERVES 6–8

50 g/2 oz soft vegetable margarine
50 g/2 oz Muscovado sugar
2 free-range eggs
75 g/3 oz wholemeal flour
75 g/3 oz ground hazelnuts
mint sprig to decorate (optional)
Topping
150 ml/¼ pint red grape juice
1½ teaspoons powdered gelatine
175 g/6 oz strawberries
1 small pineapple

■

*Preparation time **30 minutes***
*Cooking time **30 minutes***
*Chilling time **30 minutes***
*Oven temperature **170 C, 325 F, gas 3***

1 Lightly grease an 18–20-cm/7–8-in cake tin.
2 Cream together the margarine and sugar until light and fluffy.
3 Beat in the eggs, one at a time, beating well between additions.
4 Sift the flour, returning the bran in the sieve to the bowl. Fold the hazelnuts and the flour into the mixture and turn into the prepared tin. Bake for 30 minutes. Allow to cool completely before topping.
5 Heat the grape juice in a saucepan to boiling point.
6 Remove from the heat and sprinkle on the gelatine and stir until dissolved. Pour into a basin to cool.
7 Pick over the strawberries, hull and halve.
8 Peel the pineapple and cut the flesh into cubes, removing any hard pieces.
9 Arrange the strawberries and pineapple on top of the torte and spoon over the red jelly when it is on the point of setting. Refrigerate for 1 hour to chill and set. Decorate, if liked, with a sprig of mint before serving.

Strawberry and Pineapple Hazelnut Torte

Per portion:
Serves 6
Calories 270
Fat 13g
Fibre 4g
Serves 7
Calories 230
Fat 12g
Fibre 3g
Serves 8
Calories 200
Fat 10g
Fibre 2½g

Coffee and Ginger
Mousse

Coffee and Ginger Mousse	
Per portion:	
Serves 4:	
Calories 210	
Fat 4g	
Fibre 0g	
Serves 5:	
Calories 165	
Fat 4g	
Fibre 0g	
Serves 6:	
Calories 140	
Fat 3g	
Fibre 0g	

COFFEE AND
GINGER MOUSSE

SERVES 4–6

$4\frac{1}{2}$ tablespoons black decaffeinated
coffee
15 g/$\frac{1}{2}$ oz powdered gelatine
3 free-range eggs, separated
75 g/3 oz clear honey
25 g/1 oz preserved stem ginger
450 ml/$\frac{3}{4}$ pint strained natural yogurt
Decoration (optional)
$\frac{1}{2}$ teaspoon decaffeinated coffee powder
few slices preserved stem ginger

■

Preparation time **15–20 minutes**
Chilling and setting time **2 hours**

1 Have ready a 15-cm/6-in soufflé dish.
2 Make the coffee and pour it into a small bowl or cup. Sprinkle on the gelatine, stirring to dissolve it, then place on one side to cool.
3 Whisk the egg yolks and honey with an electric whisk until pale and thick.
4 Drain the stem ginger and chop very finely. Fold into egg and honey mixture.
5 Drizzle in the coffee gelatine and mix well to combine. Carefully fold in the yogurt. Whisk and fold in the egg whites. Pour into the prepared soufflé dish and refrigerate until firmly set.
6 Decorate, if liked, with a sprinkling of ground coffee and some sliced stem ginger placed around the edge of the dish.

Instead of double cream, this mousse uses natural strained yogurt for a delicious dessert that is lower in fat and calories than the usual mousses.

Baked Peaches

BAKED PEACHES

SERVES 4

4 large, juicy peaches
50 g/2 oz digestive biscuits
100 g/4 oz medium-fat curd cheese
1 free-range egg
few drops of natural bitter almond essence
150 ml/¼ pint orange and apricot juice
mint sprig to decorate

■

*Preparation time **14 minutes***
*Cooking time **20 minutes***
*Oven temperature **180 C, 350 F, gas 4***

■

1 Have ready an ovenproof dish in which the halved peaches will fit comfortably.

2 Skin the peaches: plunge them into boiling water for a minute, then place in cold water. The skins should slip off easily.

3 Halve the skinned peaches and remove the stone. Cut out a little more of the flesh to make a slightly bigger hole. Reserve the flesh.

4 Crush the biscuits to crumbs. In a basin, mix most of the crumbs, reserving some for sprinkling on top, with the cheese, egg and almond essence, then add the reserved peach flesh. Thin the mixture a little with a couple of tablespoons of the juice, if necessary. Use this mixture to stuff the peach halves.

5 Place the peach halves in a dish and pour around the rest of the juice. Sprinkle the remaining biscuit crumbs on top and bake for 20 minutes. Decorate with a sprig of mint before serving.

Baked Peaches

Per portion:

Calories 190

Fat 6g

Fibre 3g

DIETARY GOALS

The NACNE Report in 1983 pointed to a healthier way of eating and suggested we aim to make up our diet from the following balance of foods:

Protein	11 per cent (No change)
Fat	34 per cent (A reduction)
Carbohydrate	50 per cent (An increase)
Alcohol	5 per cent (A reduction)
Total:	100 per cent

We could do even better and aim for a greater percentage on the carbohydrates and much less fat. A wholefood diet might be nearer 70 per cent unrefined carbohydrates, reducing the fat to 14 per cent and making two-thirds of that fat polyunsaturated.

COMPARING CREAM AND YOGURT

Creams	Calories	% Fat
Single	212	21.2
Double	447	48.2
Clotted	578	55.6
Whipping	332	35
Soured	212	21.2

Yogurt

Natural	52	1
Fruit (average)	95	1
Strained natural	145	10
Strained natural, low-fat	80	1

HOW MUCH FAT IN YOGURT

Claim on Pot	% Fat
Low-fat	0.5–2
Very low-fat	less than 0.5
Skimmed milk yogurt	less than 0.5

HOW MUCH FAT IN MILK

	%Fat Content	Calories
Silver Top, (Pasteurised)	3.8	380
Red Top, (Homogenised)	3.8	380
Blue Top, (Sterilised)	3.8	380
Gold Top, (Channel Island)	4.8	445
Red/Silver Stripe, (Semi-skimmed)	1.5–1.8	263–280
Blue/Silver Check, (Skimmed)	0.1	195
Green Top, (Untreated or Raw)	dependent on herd	

WHOLEMEAL v WHITE FLOUR

Nutrient	Wholemeal Flour	White Flour
Fibre	9.6	3.4
Calories	318	350
Potassium	360	130
Calcium	35	150*
Iron	4	2.2
Zinc	3	0.9

Vitamins

B1	0.46	0.31
B2	0.8	0.03
Nictoinic Acid	5.6	2
E	1.6	Trace
B6	0.5	0.15
Folic Acid	57	22
Pantothenic Acid	0.8	0.3
Biotin	7	1

* Fortified by law
Source: McCance and Widdowson, *The Composition of Foods*, HMSO, 1978

WHOLEFOOD AND REFINED – SPOT THE DIFFERENCE

	Fibre	Calories
Wholemeal Bread	8.5	216
White Bread	2.7	233
Brown Rice, raw	5.5	360
White Rice, raw	3	400
Wholemeal Flour	9.6	318
White Flour	4	400

Source: McCance and Widdowson, *The Composition of Foods*, HMSO, 1978

FIBRE AND CALORIE CONTENT OF COMMON BREADS PER 100 GRAMS

	Fibre	Calories
Wholemeal	8.5	215
Hovis	5.8	211
Vitbe	6.4	252
White	4	242
French	5.6	270
Granary	7.3	235
Rye	6.4	220
White rolls, soft	4.2	268
Brown rolls, soft	7	268
Wholemeal rolls	9.7	243

Source: 'Nutritional Composition of British Breads, 1983', R. W. Wenlock *et al*, *Journal of Agriculture and Food Science*

Index